PEOPLED ECONOMIES

PEOPLED ECONOMIES

CONVERSATIONS WITH
STEPHEN GUDEMAN

EDITED BY STAFFAN LÖFVING

INTERFACE, UPPSALA 2005

ISBN 91-974705-6-2
ISSN 1652-9529

INTERFACE

Series editors
Staffan Löfving, Heidi Moksnes, and Lars Rudebeck

Design and typesetting
Vida Form, Uppsala

Language editor
Anne Cleaves

Reviewed and funded by
Swedish Research Council

Published in Sweden by
Collegium for Development Studies, Uppsala University
Övre Slottsgatan 1
SE-75310 Uppsala
http://www.kus.uu.se//

Distributed by
Almqvist & Wiksell International
P.O. Box 7634
SE-103 94 Stockholm
Sweden
Fax +46 (0)8 24 25 43
E-mail order@akademibokhandeln.se

Keywords: cultural economics, development, economy,
economic anthropology, Stephen Gudeman, post-modern
theory, interdisciplinarity

Printed in Gdansk, Poland, by Förlags ab Gondolin.

CONTENTS

PREFACE

INTERFACE is a forum for transdisciplinary exchanges of research and scholarly curiosity. It aims at critically exploring issues traditionally associated with the field of development studies. Individual articles and theme-oriented volumes engage with a variety of theoretical debates in social science and the humanities. We encourage an open dialogue between scholars with different experiences of life and research on topics such as colonialism, democracy, economy, ethnicity, feminism, geo-politics, globalization, imperialism, nationalism, poverty, rights, violence, and the past and future of the division between so-called first and third world countries and concerns.

INTERFACE is published by the Seminar for Development Studies – a meeting place within the Collegium for Development Studies, Uppsala University, for researchers and students with a shared interest in issues of society and development.

This first INTERFACE volume is the outcome of a seminar held in the spring of 2003, called *Cultural Economics: A Critical Assessment*. It acknowledged the need for new analytical approaches to the study of development, globalization and the field of economy itself amidst dramatic changes in local and global economies, as well as in the very relationships between them. In the seminar, renowned economic anthropologist, Stephen Gudeman, who, at the time, was visiting researcher at SCASSS – the Swedish Collegium for Advanced Study in the Social Sciences – discussed his much acclaimed *The Anthropology of Economy* (Blackwell 2001) with a board of reviewers, representing perspectives from philosophy, anthropology and economics. Gudeman argued that, across cultures, economy can be understood as a combination of communal processes and market forces. Drawing from a wide range of intellectual sources he approached the emergence and distribution of profit, the effects of expanding capital on marginalized groups, and, also, people's shifting identities in response to the growth of the global market. Some of his views were embraced and applauded, others vociferously challenged.

The economic support for *Peopled Economies* by the Swedish Research Council and the insightful reading by its anonymous reviewer are gratefully acknowledged. We also thank the participants in the 2003 seminar and note with delight that the conversation on the critical assessment of cultural economics goes on.

The INTERFACE Series editors,
Uppsala, May 2005.

INTRODUCTION

PEOPLED ECONOMIES

STAFFAN LÖFVING

What is the relation between culture and economy? Are they separate slices of life, such as beliefs versus action or meaning versus mechanistics? Are they intertwined or does one determine the other? These questions have long animated the encounter between anthropology and economics, which view each other uneasily across their borders. Today variations of the culture/economy question weave across many disciplines and have provoked, at least partly, a divide between humanistic and social-science approaches. The theme has practical importance, too, for in conditions of environmental deterioration, increasing expansion of poverty, and growing disparities of wealth within and between nations, there are many calls for rethinking what we mean by "development," and the way we conduct economic life.

The contributions to this volume focus on this central contemporary issue, but in a unique way. The contributors, who represent different disciplines and very different perspectives, are joined in a debate and sometimes fractious confrontation. In order that readers may see the clarity of the positions and the conviction with which they are held, no voices have been smoothed or volumes lowered. The discussion began as an interdisciplinary conference that was held at Uppsala University in 2003 and organized around the recent book by Stephen Gudeman, *The Anthropology of Economy* (2001a), a theoretically innovative and much-acclaimed monograph (see, e.g., Gregory 2002). In addition to Gudeman, an anthropologist, the conference included accomplished scholars from related fields. Gert Helgesson is a philosopher with special interests in epistemology and economics. Lars Pålsson Syll is an economic historian who embraces an institutional approach to economy. Alf Hornborg is also an anthropologist with longstanding concerns in ecology. The commentators were asked to use Gudeman's book as a point of departure for the presentation of their own perspective. The subsequent discussion was very heated, enlightening, and frequently surprising. Here, it was the philosopher who most agreed with Gudeman and the anthropologist who most disagreed with him, while the economic historian did a bit of both. Gudeman's response to the commentators extends his work and provides a conclusion to this volume. We view this book as one part of a long conversation that may help reveal the excitement and clarity that come when engaged scholars cross disciplinary boundaries, talk to one another, and ardently disagree.

In the remainder of this introduction I discuss some of the implications of our conversation for "development" studies and the relation between economics and anthropology, before turning to a review of Gudeman's work as background for the reader. I end with a discussion of the dilemmas and promises of transdisciplinary encounters.[1]

CULTURE AND ECONOMY

Inspired by the challenge posed by the interface between culture and economy in development studies, two World Bank economists recently assembled leading economists and anthropologists for an interdisciplinary exchange of ideas and experiences.[2] Motivated to find "a middle way" between those who see culture as an obstacle to neoliberal development (e.g., Harrison and Huntington 2000) and those who would undermine a policy-oriented economistic approach by exploring development itself as a cultural system of meaning and exploitation (e.g., Ferguson 1990; Escobar 1995), the conference aimed at opening a dialogue about political measures to alleviate poverty and see cultural variation as something other than an exogenous constraint (Rao and Walton 2004).

The urgent need for such an approach stems from a problematic dominance within development economics

---

[1] I gratefully acknowledge the constructive criticism Michael Barrett, Stephen Gudeman, and Lars Rudebeck gave to earlier drafts of this introduction. I am grateful also to Harald Runblom and the Centre for Multiethnic Research at Uppsala University for the moral and practical support without which this project would not have been accomplished.

[2] Proceedings with links and commentaries are available on http://www.cultureandpublicaction.org// and the papers are published in the volume *Culture and Public Action*, edited by Vijayendra Rao and Michael Walton, Stanford University Press, 2004.

of a market-oriented neoclassical approach to poverty alleviation (see, e.g., www.wider.unu.edu). "Development economics nowadays is mainstream economics applied to poor countries" writes Kanbur (2002:477), who adds that while the theoretical advancements in mainstream economics do grapple with the social norms that determine and change preferences and behaviors, and with the problematically changing and culturally constituted concept of the household, most "policy economists, including policy development economists, seem by and large to be innocent of these writings" (ibid.). Past surveys of research in the field of development economics (see, e.g., Bardhan 1989; Stern 1989; Lodewijks 1994) reveal the longer history of this state of affairs. The remedy proposed by Kanbur, much like Rao and Walton's, consists in a serious commitment to a multidisciplinary approach to economy.

But how serious can we be, and what does seriousness in this case actually entail? Our volume offers a different project. Instead of exploring if the two domains of knowledge and practice represented by economy and culture, and the analytical tools provided by economics and anthropology respectively, actually fit together, we ask what perpetuates this difference and what it means for the production of knowledge about people whose lives are seriously constrained by poverty, which returns us to the culture/economy interface, or the one between the academic disciplines themselves (cf. Friedland and Robertson 1990).

The Rao and Walton conference and their publication of its papers is an attempt at bridging a deeply entrenched divide, and it is hardly representative of contemporary conversations either within anthropology and economics or between the two fields. It shows that what are perceived today as peripheral discussions within monolithic disciplines – the intellectual borderland where economy turns into culture and culture into economy – might reflect something central in people's lives and realities. From a position within their respective disciplines, the contributors to this present volume converse their way towards an understanding of the mundane practices of production, distribution, and exchange that we have assembled under the novel rubric of "peopled economies." That concept is not borrowed from economic anthropology, but is inspired by it, and in particular by Gudeman's re-conceptualization of economy as that particular practice which evolves around the dialectic of market and community.

The social and cultural dimensions of economy are phenomena allegedly devoid of context-specific meaning and variation in dominant discourses on things economic. In daily speech, we sometimes even use the term "economic" when alluding to the raw, impersonal, or technical aspects of behavior and relationships. *Homo economicus* is not a particularly social character, but a self-absorbed agent occupied by the cynicism (or efficiencies, depending on one's political leaning) of individual gain.[3] Such a perception is partly rooted in the formation of Western science and assumed the status of dogma in ne-

---

[3] See Saumitra Jah's "Cultured Economic Theory: Oxymoron or Incipient Reality?" (2004) for a contrasting view.

oclassical economics (Harriss 2002). There *the market* constitutes the sole domain of value, in turn built up by the institutions of the household and the business between which materials, goods, and services are circularly exchanged. Everything can be priced in this domain, which means that what cannot, like various forms of *communal transactions*, is silenced. Writes Stephen Gudeman:

> [They] represent irrationalities, frictions, hindrances, or 'externalities' to a system that is otherwise efficient. In this discourse [on economy], efficiency is the central value, while 'development' broadly means replacing 'old' with 'new' values by bringing the market realm to prominence through new legal structures .... (2001a:6)

By turning their gaze towards Western or "first world" societies, anthropologists have shown that people professing a rational culture (if any culture at all) are not necessarily more rational than others (see, e.g., Hornborg 1993 and 2001); quite the opposite! Those who cherish *rationality* reveal remarkably *irrational* features. For instance, the rise to power of global capital has turned economic experts into diviners in the contemporary world of profane power (see Rappaport 1999; Bowles 1998; Gudeman 2001a:107). A critical observer might say that economists, like meteorologists, have their séances on televised news, predicting the future (recession and rain, falling interest rates and high pressure) and ritually putting the world of the viewers back in order, re-assembling their pieces of hope shattered by the mediated chaos of unpredictable politics (and weather systems).

This paradox, then – economics as "the queen of the social sciences" (Samuelson 1997; see Cullenberg, Amariglio and Ruccio 2001:39n2) modeling a market devoid of social disturbance on the one hand, and the magic by which economic predictions become politically self-fulfilling prophecies on the other – electrifies the very topic of economy and makes conversations about it anything but value-free. I would even suggest that in an age of moral extremism when nations, cultures, and religions are rhetorically attached to axes of good and evil, this ambivalent role of economy in society positions it too as one of our most contested domains of knowledge (see Hutchison 1977; Hart 2000).

Culture, on the other hand, what it is and how it should be handled in science and politics, is hardly an easier nut to crack than economy. A comparison of the two in popular Western imagination reveals some interesting characteristics. Whereas economics has become the science of the future, anthropology with its focus on culture is associated with the past (Appadurai 2004). The culture connotations of habit, custom, heritage, and tradition account for this view in the same way that wants, needs, expectations, and calculations speak to the futurity of economics. No wonder, then, that development has become the domain of economists and not of anthropologists!

Some voices within the disciplines do offer alternative conceptualizations. Neoclassical orthodoxy has been exposed to critical scrutiny within economics itself. Many of the criticisms that challenge the modernist notions of evolution and scientific progress would see economic knowledge as a set of models emerging in a particular cultural context (see, e.g., Tribe 1978; McCloskey 1985 and 1994; Resnick and Wolff 1987; Cullenberg, Amariglio and Ruccio 2001). Similarly, the "custom and tradition" understanding of culture has long been abandoned or supplemented in anthropology. This is not the place to dwell on the contested meanings of the most central concept in twentieth-century anthropology. Suffice it to say that an essentialist usage of culture has been re-evaluated, leading to the use of the adjective "cultural" instead of the noun "culture" and to associating it with dynamic processes of meaning-making and the construction of social difference. Arjun Appadurai's explicit attempt at making the culture concept useful in development practice engages culture in terms of people's capacity to *aspire*. "As far back as Emile Durkheim and George Herbert Mead, we have learned that there is no self outside a social frame, setting, and mirror. Could it be otherwise for aspirations?" (Appadurai 2004:67). In a similar vein, sociologist Ghassan Hage has moved away from older definitions of society and has proposed one that centers on future prospects. The health of society, according to him, can be measured by its ability to distribute *hope* (Hage 2003).´

ECONOMIC ANTHROPOLOGY ACCORDING TO GUDEMAN

Stephen Gudeman is one of the leading economic anthropologists of our time. His bibliography, the major publications of which are compiled in the reference list of this introduction, spans five books and a vast number of articles either preparing the more fully developed theories of each book, or applying the models and perspectives of the respective books to new cultural contexts. Here I will attempt to trace the intellectual thread of his work by focusing on Gudeman's treatment over time of the concepts of the subtitle of his most recent book, namely *community*, *market*, and *culture*.

The archetypal anthropologist, true to the traditions of the discipline, explores the local aspect of the human condition. The locality in question, which has either been the context of the subject matter, or the subject matter itself, particularly in writings on Latin America, is *the community* – peasant or later labeled indigenous.[4] During the years of Gudeman's first studies, an older view of the community as a social sphere in political and economic isolation was giving way to a Marxist-inspired realization that modernization turned "noble savages" into wage laborers and that isolation was one of the fundaments of colonial mythmaking. In *Relationships, Residence and the Individual: A Rural Panamanian Community* (1976), Gudeman advanced the thinking of the time by combining extended anthropological fieldwork in a Panamanian village with dependency school theories, Marxism, and neo-Ricardian economics. His own training as an econo-

[4] See, for example, Polly Hill's *Development Economics on Trial: The Anthropological Case for a Prosecution*, Cambridge, 1986, for a relativist critique of the allegedly universal category of the peasant, and Michael Kearney's *Reconceptualizing the Peasantry: Anthropology in Global Perspective*, Westview, 1996, in which the author approaches the turn to identity and self-representation in what he calls the "post-peasant" era.

mist reveals itself in the form of an interest in "the individual" within the larger society. Following the non-evolutionist strands of Marcel Mauss's work on persons as culturally elaborated roles assigned to individuals in society (see Carrithers 1996), Gudeman argued that even though human beings constitute the empirical objects of society everywhere, the way in which individuals are *conceptualized* differs as societies differ. By studying how rights and responsibilities are attached to these roles with reference to sex, age, kinship, and friendship positions (among others), an anthropological approach to individuals can unravel the culturally specific construction of what in neoclassical economics is referred to in terms of universal "preferences" and "needs" (see Helgesson in this volume). But this was not the sole, nor even the main aim of his anthropological approach to persons in society. Instead, his contribution in 1976 focused on the interplay of individuals and systems of relationships. Gudeman showed how individuals, by paying "respect" (a local idea) to others who played their roles well within society, also paid respect to the system itself.

The notion of community in these early writings was thus centered more on the perpetuation of social relationships than on the meaning of history and heritage, and on place and natural habitat. What changed as Gudeman took on the larger issues of capitalist penetration of rural communities in the Panamanian sequel to his debut – published in 1978 as *The Demise of a Rural Economy: From Subsistence to Capitalism in a Latin American Village* – was the exposure of seemingly perpetual structures of communal relationships to the forces of world trade.[5] Gudeman entered this problematique through the gates of economy. His focus was on the transition from subsistence farming (rice and maize) to cash cropping (sugar cane) gradually resulting in a total transformation of people's economy and, by Gudemanian implication, also their community.

The debate between the formalists and the substantivists had long dominated economic anthropology, and Gudeman explicitly sought to transcend what he viewed as the dead end of the sub-discipline. This debate began when the economic historian Karl Polanyi drew on Menger and Weber's distinction between formal and substantive rationality to explore the main cleavage in social scientific approaches to economy. Whereas the *formal* approach resembled that of modern economics and focused on the rationality that people employ when confronted with different choices, the *substantive* definition of economy had a much wider scope. It was aimed at the study of societies where economy was still seen as being closely connected to other "social things" such as kinship, religion, and politics (Polanyi 1957). The ensuing debate between the adherents of these two approaches (see Leclair and Schneider 1968) dominated economic anthropology until the emergence of a Marxist approach which, like that of the substantivists, questioned an allegedly value-free Western economics but turned out to be as universalist and insensitive to cultural variation as the formalists it critiqued. Gudeman writes in 1978:

[5] See the discussion of Mary Douglas in Rao and Walton 2004:88–89.

> The debate between the formalists and the substan-
> tivists, that acrimonious discussion frequently unre-
> lated to ethnographic facts, has ... numbed the entire
> field .... The substantivists may have over-emphasised
> the domain of transactions, but the byway of the for-
> malists is more treacherous, for they have abstracted
> from the entire history of economic thought one pe-
> riod, which lies roughly between Marx and Keynes,
> and raised it to the level of universality. (1978b:1)

What emerges in *The Demise of a Rural Economy* as
an alternative, or a third (or fourth) way for economic
anthropology is a move away from the focus of both formalists and substantivists in order to explore what determines value and distribution. Whereas the neoclassical
(formalist) approach to this question emphasizes exchange in an unrestricted (or "free") market where supply and demand determines the value of goods and of
labor, the followers of Ricardo and Marx argue that market transactions are *preceded* by a class distribution of
resources. The determination of value is thus to be found
in the process of production, not in the process of exchange. What Gudeman wanted to do with this was to
reclaim the debate "as an anthropologist" and to explore
the importance of social life for the issue of distribution.
With that, he sided with the neo-Ricardians, but more
importantly he advanced the agenda by re-conceptualiz-
ing economy in terms of a fundamentally social aspect of
human life:

> If, then, distribution is treated as an initial datum and
> not as an outcome of the market or reciprocity or re-
> distribution, the emphasis of the analysis must shift

from the sphere of exchange to production, and beyond that to the socio-cultural conditions in which
the production process itself takes place. It follows
that the anthropologist has a unique contribution to
offer to the unravelling of the seemingly "economic"
problem of distribution. (1978b:5; cf. Gudeman
1978a)

The community, however, even if entangled in webs
of dependency, remained a geographically confined entity in the sense that social relationships built on face-to-
face interaction. Gudeman thus had yet to develop the
dialectics between market and community, since here, a
growing market seemed to be depending on "consumption" and thereby destruction of community itself.

Over the course of some three decades of research
and writing, Gudeman's conception of the community
as such seems to have lost this implicit attachment to
specific territories. This is beautifully captured in the 1990
volume called *Conversations in Colombia: The Domestic
Economy in Life and Text*, written with his friend and
former student Alberto Rivera. The authors argue that
both local farmers and theoreticians like themselves are
engaged in conversations that bridge times and places,
thus creating "conversational communities" (cf. McCloskey 1985). Central to Gudeman and Rivera is the rejec-
tion of a scientific hegemony that, while it has acknowledged the fact that economists and theoreticians are
modelers as opposed to Enlightened Truth-Tellers, reserves
the act of modeling for scientific work (i.e., that of economists) exclusively. In their rendering, modeling is not
opposed to the practices the models are aimed at explain-

ing. Instead, "[F]olk have economic models, too" (Gudeman and Rivera 1990:189):

> [P]ractice refers to the actions and voices of people in history that are sometimes inscribed in texts and of which the inscription is itself an example. We find it useful to talk about all this – the practice, the inscribing, the text, and its readings – as a long conversation in which folk, inscribers, readers, and listeners are all engaged. (ibid.)

Writes Keith Hart:

> *Conversations in Colombia* (1990) demonstrates that a commitment both to ethnography and to the history of economic ideas should be indispensable to the serious practice of this subdiscipline. [Gudeman and Rivera] argue convincingly that economic traditions we know only through the abstractions of dead texts live on in the marginal peasantries of the Third World. (2000:1023)

To this reader, *Conversations in Colombia* represents an intellectual peak in the development (or should we say "emergence") of postmodern anthropology. One characteristic of the postmodern turn within the discipline has been a shift away from the ethnography of exotic others to the ethnography of adjacent others within the ethnographer's own society (Nugent 1996). Gudeman's work represents a variation on this theme since, by writing about and demystifying the exotic other, his ethnographies become texts in which we can mirror "ourselves." They are thus challenging anthropology's longstanding tradition of being the science par excellence of otherness.

The reflexivity of postmodernism has remained a contested issue in anthropology over the last fifteen years, much due to the fact that its methodology revolves around fieldwork where anthropologists have claimed an exclusive access to a reality irreducible to text, perspective, and surface. Again, Stephen Gudeman's contribution breaks new ground in that it discovers or unravels the textuality of, and the conflicting discourses among, those who have previously been conceived of as authentic, exotic, or primitive. The ethnographic fieldwork professed by Gudeman becomes an exercise in inter-textual analysis.

What glues communities together, then, when place does not, is something that Gudeman explains by using the Latin American term "the base" (see Gudeman and Rivera 1990:54–83; Gudeman 2001a:25–67, 80–93). The base differs from cultural and social capital[6] and from the commons in that it consists of incommensurate things that cannot be valued according to one measuring rod. The base thus resists commoditization.

Now, we have already paid a visit to the relation of market to community and seen how it appeared as one of mutual exclusiveness in *The Demise of a Rural Econo-*

---

[6] Robert Putnam's influential discussion on trust as product of accumulated social capital (see Putnam et al. 1992 and Putnam 2000) bears a resemblance to Gudeman's notion of the base, but for Putnam, Gudeman argues, "dyadic ties provide the foundations for material life, and so the broader communal commitments from which they derive are obscured" (Gudeman 2001a:19). See Helgesson in this volume, pages 39–45.

my in 1978. Less has been said about the dialectics of Gudeman's more recent model.

Market, in the singular, "designates anonymous, short-term exchanges" (Gudeman 2001a:1) and "market trade revolves about exchange value or increasing monetary capital" (ibid.:11). In contrast, communal trade secures goods that sustain the base and involves already existing relationships that do not come into being due to nor depend entirely on the trade in question. Market systems need the support of the communal realm – "shared languages, mutual ways of interacting, and implicit understandings" (ibid.). The market can draw a surplus from a community economy,

> when subsistence farming supports cash cropping or when people undertake piecework or telemarketing from their homes at very low rates of remuneration. In the West, too, there has been a long term shift from community to market that is often described as modernization, progress, and the triumph of rationality. (ibid.)

The community realm thus seems to be less dependent on the market than the other way around, but Gudeman locates the dialectics in their long-term relationship:

> For example, the emergence of household-based trade on the margins of growing markets – as in the rise of informal economy – may be a dialectical response to the centralization of economic power, the growth of monopolistic practices, and state control (Hart 1992). (ibid.:12)

The conversation of Lars Pålsson Syll and Stephen

Gudeman in this volume gets down to the nitty-gritty of the market realm, first explored by Gudeman in the chapter called "Trade and Profit" (2001a:94–109). Suffice it to mention here that the role of the market within contemporary societies that we sketched in one of the first paragraphs to this introduction is another example of when and how the community realm "consumes" the market, to the eventual reinforcement of both:

> Given the important place of economics in Western societies, the dividing line between market fact and market model ... is thin, because models of economic behavior ... affect market performance just as its everyday operations and changes influence theory.... (ibid.:94)

Despite the fact that culture appears in its very subtitle, *The Anthropology of Economy* refrains from using the culture concept except in the adjective (see above). Thus, *cultural* categories are those with which commensuration is accomplished (making money a cultural category) (ibid.:12–15); *cultural* transfer occurs when a U.S. entrepreneur, through his access to capital, uses the historical innovations and labor skills of highland Guatemalan women for private benefit (ibid.:117–118); and the *cultural* models of the base emerge from the world of – sometimes past but always particular and shared – experience (ibid.:34). *Cultural* economics, finally, becomes a comprehensive labeling of that which is explored in much more detail in terms of market-community dialectics.

The 1986 volume *Economics as Culture: Models and Metaphors of Livelihood* is a compilation of parts of previously published chapters and articles (see Gudeman 1979, 1980 and 1984) and five new chapters, all of which explore specific theoretical issues. If the studies of the 1970s ethnographically encompassed a historical and cultural context, it is in the 1986 publication that the author breaks free from the monograph form and endeavors a comparative project in the development of a theoretical model. By deconstructing Western categories of knowledge Gudeman reveals the chimera of universal models in economics, tracing their roots to local constructions in the history of economic thought. Such an endeavor does not pass unnoticed, and it is interesting to note the very different reception this book got among admiring anthropologists on the one hand (see, e.g., Hornborg in this volume) and apparently disturbed economists on the other (see, e.g., Stanfield 1988). He elaborates this theme in our volume.

In our résumé, we have now reached the model of Gudeman's most recent book, where economy consists of two realms or spheres. Gudeman labels them "market" and "community." This contrasts with views among economists that market and economy are synonymous and that there is nothing – or *should* be nothing – to complicate that equivalence. "The more market driven, the better the economy," so the mainstream neoclassical argument goes. Economic transformations, what has been described in the West as modernization, is, in fact, a shift from the community realm to that of the market.

The concept of value is elevated to one of the core elements of Gudeman's model. For the mainstream economist, market and economy have one value, but if the

Marxist approaches this single value in terms of labor, the neoclassical economist uses utility theory. The economic agent was, for the Marxist, the industrial worker who produced a surplus for the owner of the industry. In the neoclassical view that became dominant after the 1970s, the agent was rather the individual consumer. But Gudeman argues that neither of these approaches is able to get to the core of economic activities. He therefore proposes a fourfold and more complex division of value into the domains of, first, the base (locally defined values related to the identity of the members of a specific community – land, water, embodied goods, ideology, etc.); second, social relationships and associations (connections maintained for their own sake, not for the sake of profit, like house economies, and nations); third, goods and services (traded for production or saving and consumption); and fourth and finally, appropriation and accumulation of wealth (the collecting of value).

This model of two realms and four value domains enhances an understanding of both economic agency and economic change in new and radical ways. If the community realm and the value domains of the base and of social relationships enable us to see economic agency in production for domestic use, in gift exchanges, and in godparenthood, for example, then the transformation from that realm and those domains to the incommensurate realm of the market and the domains of trade and accumulation sheds light on the nature of economic changes and on how global markets transform not only the material conditions of human existence, but also, and as a consequence, our identities. Gudeman's re-conceptualization could thus be employed in the analysis of contemporary phenomena like environmental degradation with its cargo of social fragmentation, resulting from privatizations that turn land and water from the value domain of the base to that of appropriation. Gudeman rhetorically asks if development policies should aim at restructuring societies in the name of the market, or if, instead, emphasis should be placed on community – on strengthening the value domain of the base in order for people to become innovators (cf. Gudeman 2004b). He argues that profit starts with innovation – a creation of value dependent on community, since what is produced when innovation occurs is not just goods and services but also a relation to others.

THE INTERDISCIPLINARY ENCOUNTER

In many pleas for encounters across the disciplines one finds the notion, often explicit and sometimes implicit, that the disciplines possess strengths which, when added to the strength of other disciplines, will account for a new whole, and a more complete scientific project. This perspective dates back to a time when the civilized world became equipped with academic observers of its own economy, religion, history, and so on, and anthropologists were allotted that which remained beyond civilization. "[F]or better or for worse," writes Heath Pearson, "the twentieth century witnessed the progressive estrangement of the social and behavioral sciences" (2000:972). Economics played a leading role in this process, since "price theory" was the centerpiece of the neoclassical turn and since it could not be employed in the study of societies without monetary markets. Eric Wolf goes further back, pointing to a critical turning point around the middle of the nineteenth century,

> when enquiry into the nature and varieties of human-kind split into separate (and unequal) specialties and disciplines. ... [T]he severance of social relations from the economic, political and ideological contexts in which they are embedded and which they activate was accompanied by the assignment of the economic and political aspects of human life to separate disciplines. (1982:7–9)

John Harriss interestingly evokes the double connotation of *discipline* in the English language, derived from "disciple" and "meaning." On the one hand it refers to the training of scholars and on the other to a system of rules for conduct and order maintained among persons under control or command. Discipline is thus both something productive and something repressive, and even though the disciplinary division of work and knowledge within academe allegedly enjoys the status of the former,[7] it should be clear by now that an understanding of peopled economies has been hampered, if not suppressed, by academic divisions. It is thus central to the methodology proposed in this volume that scholars engage in conversations that bridge such divisions.

One discovery as we went down this path was that a particular discipline might certainly not be the sole in-

---

[7] See Hornborg's and Pålsson Syll's "defenses" of the intellectual perspectives of their respective disciplines in this volume.

fluence on a scholar's perspective, and that views and standpoints are less inclined to conform to disciplinary dogmas than some of us had expected. A skeptical reader might object that one scholar cannot represent a scientific discipline, but that is exactly our point. The idea of adding others for the purpose of "supplementing" the views of these authors would expose a hidden notion of bounded disciplines, of which "average scholars" could be spokespersons. Our take is different: An economist would certainly have introduced this volume in a different way, but Gudeman and Hornborg's argument on the following pages teaches us that so would another anthropologist.

I end with a quote from Gudeman and Rivera, a recipe for transdisciplinary conversations not, as in *Peopled Economies*, limited to the world of academics:

> [O]ne purpose of anthropology is to bring to the bar of discussion different conversations in space and history. This principled starting place is just the reverse of that of other disciplines. Much of modern economics, for example, starts from a Cartesian ego or from a reified model of the individual from which behaviour in any aggregate is deduced; much has been lost by effacing the vocal presence of the other, and if we are once again to take cognizance of human experience, daily lives, and the shifting problems of survival – whether in the rural areas of Colombia or the peripheries of the market in modern cities – we must expand our conversation to include other communities of people, their practices and their voices, which, to judge by Colombia, are sometimes not so different from our own. (1990:191)

Now, let the conversations begin!

REFERENCES

Appadurai, Arjun. 2004. "The Capacity to Aspire: Culture and the Terms of Recognition," *Culture and Public Action*, ed. Vijayendra Rao and Michael Walton, pp. 59–84. Stanford: Stanford University Press.

Bardhan, Pranab (ed.). 1989. *Conversations between Economists and Anthropologists: Methodological Issues in Measuring Economic Change in Rural India*. Delhi: Oxford University Press.

Bowles, Samuel. 1998. "Endogenous Preferences: The Cultural Consequences of Markets and Other Economic Institutions," *Journal of Economic Literature*, vol. XXXVI, pp. 75–111.

Carrithers, Michael. 1996. "Person," *Encyclopaedia of Social and Cultural Anthropology*, ed. Allan Barnard and Jonathan Spencer, pp. 419–423. London: Routledge.

Cullenberg, Stephen, Jack Amariglio and David F. Ruccio (eds.). 2001. *Postmodernism, Economics and Knowledge*. London: Routledge.

Douglas, Mary. 2004. "Traditional Culture – Let's Hear No More About It," *Culture and Public Action*, ed. Vijayendra Rao and Michael Walton, pp. 85–109. Stanford: Stanford University Press.

Escobar, Arturo. 1995. *Encountering Development: The Making and Unmaking of the Third World*. Princeton: Princeton University Press.

Ferguson, James. 1990. *The Anti-politics Machine: "Development," Depoliticization, and Bureaucratic Power in Lesotho*. Cambridge: Cambridge University Press.

Friedland, Roger, and Alexander F. Robertson. (eds.). 1990. *Beyond the Marketplace: Rethinking Economy and Society*. New York: Aldine de Gruyter.

Gregory, Chris. 2002. "Review," *The Australian Journal of Anthropology*, vol. 13, no. 3, pp. 361–362.

Gudeman, Stephen. 1972. "The Compadrazgo as a Reflection of the Natural and Spiritual Person," *Proceedings of the Royal Anthropological Institute for 1971*, pp. 45–71.

—. 1975. "Spiritual Relationships and Selecting a Godparent," *Man* (N.S.), vol. 10, no. 2, pp. 221–237.

—. 1976a. *Relationships, Residence and the Individual: A Ru-*

ral Panamanian Community. London: Routledge & Kegan Paul.

—. 1976b. "Saints, Symbols, and Ceremonies," *American Ethnologist*, vol. 3, pp. 709–729.

—. 1978a. "Anthropological Economics: The Question of Distribution," *Annual Review of Anthropology*, vol. 7, pp. 347–379.

—. 1978b. *The Demise of a Rural Economy: From Subsistence to Capitalism in a Latin American Village*. Boston: Routledge & Kegan Paul.

—. 1979. "Mapping Means," *Social Anthropology of Work*, ed. Sandra Wallman, pp. 229–247. London: Academic Press.

—. 1980. "Physiocracy: A Natural Economics," *American Ethnologist*, vol. 7, pp. 240–258.

—. 1984. "Ricardo's Representations," *Representations*, vol. 5. Berkeley: University of California Press.

—. 1986. *Economics as Culture: Models and Metaphors of Livelihood*. London: Routledge & Kegan Paul.

—. 1992. "Remodelling the House of Economics: Culture and Innovation," *American Ethnologist*, vol. 19, no. 1, pp. 141–154. [1991 American Ethnological Society Distinguished Lecture.]

—. 1996. "Economic Anthropology," *Encyclopedia of Social and Cultural Anthropology*, ed. Allan Barnard and Jonathan Spencer, pp. 172–178. London: Routledge.

—, ed. 1998. *Economic Anthropology*. Cheltenham: Edward Elgar Publishing Limited.

—. 2001a. *The Anthropology of Economy: Community, Market, and Culture*. Oxford: Blackwell Publishing.

—. 2001b. "Postmodern Gifts. *Postmodernism, Economics and Knowledge*, eds. Stephen Cullenberg, Jack Amariglio and David F. Ruccio, pp. 459–474. London: Routledge.

—. 2004a. "Anthropology, Economics and Development: Cross Disciplines," www.cultureandpublicaction.org

—. 2004b. "Commentary on Zen and Appadurai," www.cultureandpublicaction.org

Gudeman, Stephen, and Mischa Penn. 1982. "Models, Meaning and Reflexivity," *Semantic Anthropology*, ed. David Parkin, pp. 89–106. London: Academic Press.

Gudeman, Stephen, and Alberto Rivera-Gutiérrez. 1989.

"Colombian Conversations: The Strength of the Earth," *Current Anthropology*, vol. 30, no. 3, pp. 267–281.

—. 1990. *Conversations in Colombia: The Domestic Economy in Life and Text*. Cambridge: Cambridge University Press.

—. 1995. "From Car to House (Del coche a la casa)," *American Anthropologist*, vol. 97, no. 2, pp. 242–250.

—. 2001. "Sustaining the Community, Resisting the Market: Guatemalan Perspectives," *Land, Property and the Environment*, ed. John F. Richards, pp. 355–381. Oakland: ICS Press.

—. 2002. "Neither Duck nor Rabbit: Sustainability, Political Economy, and the Dialectics of Economy," *The Spaces of Neoliberalism in Latin America*, ed. Jacquelyn Chase, pp. 159–186. Bloomfield: Kumarian Press.

Hage, Ghassan. 2003. *Against Paranoid Nationalism: Searching for Hope in a Shrinking Society*. Annandale: Pluto Press.

Harrison, Lawrence E., and Samuel P. Huntington (eds.). 2000. *Culture Matters: How Values Shape Human Progress*. New York: Basic Books.

Harriss, John. 2002. "The Case for Cross-Disciplinary Approaches in International Development," *World Development*, vol. 30, no. 3, pp. 487–96.

Hart, Keith. 1992. "Market and State after the Cold War: The Informal Economy Reconsidered," *Contesting Markets: Analyses of Ideology, Discourse, and Practice*, ed. Roy Dilley, pp. 214–230. Edinburgh: Edinburgh University Press.

—. 2000. "Comment on Pearson's '*Homo Economicus* Goes Native,'" *History of Political Economy*, vol. 32, no. 4, pp. 1017–1025.

Hill, Polly. 1986. *Development Economics on Trial: The Anthropological Case for a Prosecution*. Cambridge: Cambridge University Press.

Hornborg, Alf. 1993. "Distinctions That Mystify: Technology versus Economy and Other Fragmentations," *Knowledge & Policy*, vol. 6, no. 2, pp. 37–46.

—. 2001. "Symbolic Technologies: Machines and the Marxian Notion of Fetishism," *Anthropological Theory*, vol. 1, no. 4, pp. 473–496.

Hutchison, Terence Wilmot. 1977. *Knowledge and Ignorance in Economics*. Chicago: University of Chicago Press.

Jha, Saumitra. 2004. "Cultured Economic Theory: Oxymoron or Incipient Reality?" www.cultureandpublicaction.org.

Kanbur, Ravi. 2002. "Economics, Social Science and Development," *World Development*, vol. 30, no. 3, pp. 477–486.

Kearney, Michael. 1996. *Reconceptualizing the Peasantry: Anthropology in Global Perspective*. Boulder: Westview.

Leclair, Edward E., and Harold K. Schneider (eds.). 1968. *Economic Anthropology: Readings in Theory and Analysis*. New York: Holt, Rinehart and Winston.

Lodewijks, John. 1994. "Anthropologists and Economists: Conflict or Cooperation?" *The Journal of Economic Methodology*, vol. 1, pp. 81–104.

McCloskey, Deirdre N. 1985. *The Rhetoric of Economics*. Madison: University of Wisconsin Press.

—. 1994. *Knowledge and Persuasion in Economics*. Cambridge: Cambridge University Press.

Nugent, Stephen. 1996. "Postmodernism," *Encyclopaedia of Social and Cultural Anthropology*, ed. Allan Barnard and Jonathan Spencer, pp. 442–444. London: Routledge.

Pearson, Heath. 2000. "*Homo Economicus* Goes Native, 1859-1945: The Rise and Fall of Primitive Economics," *History of Political Economy*, vol. 32, no. 4, pp. 933–989.

Polanyi, Karl. 1957. "The Economy as Instituted Process," *Trade and Market in the Early Empires: Economies in History and Theory*, eds. Karl Polanyi, Conrad M. Arensberg and Harri W. Pearson, pp. 243–270. Glencoe, Illinois: Free Press.

Putnam, Robert D. with Robert Leonardi and Raffaella Y. Nanetti. 1992. *Making Democracy Work: Civic Traditions in Modern Italy*. Princeton: Princeton University Press.

Putnam, Robert D. 2000. *Bowling Alone: The Collapse and Revival of American Community*. New York: Simon and Schuster.

Rao, Vijayendra, and Michael Walton. 2004. *Culture and Public Action*. Stanford: Stanford University Press.

Rappaport, Roy. 1999. *Ritual and Religion in the Making of Humanity*. Cambridge: Cambridge University Press.

Resnick, Stephen A., and Richard D. Wolff. 1987. *Knowledge and Class: A Marxian Critique of Political Economy*. Chicago: University of Chicago Press.

Samuelson, Paul. A. 1997. "Credo of a Lucky Textbook Author," *The Journal of Economic Perspectives*, vol. 11, pp. 153–160.

Stanfield, James Ronald. 1988. "Review," *Journal of Economic Issues*, vol. 22, no. 1, pp. 279–281.

Stern, Nicolas. 1989. "The Economics of Development: A Survey," *The Economic Journal*, vol. 99, pp. 597–685.

Tribe, Keith. 1978. *Land, Labour and Economic Discourse*. London: Routledge & Kegan Paul.

Wolf, Eric. 1982. *Europe and the People without History*. Berkeley: University of California Press.

RATIONALITY IN ECONOMY

AN INTERDISCIPLINARY DISPUTE

GERT HELGESSON

Neoclassical microeconomics is the dominating theoretical approach to economics, and it also greatly affects the thinking about real economies in many parts of the world, in business, politics, and elsewhere. Its influence in the "Western world" is obvious, and the World Bank and the International Monetary Fund (IMF) have imposed a neoclassical view of economic issues on a large number of countries, often by conditioning loans on institutional changes (see, e.g., George and Sabelli 1994).

The core ideas of neoclassical economics are quite simple, and this is probably an important factor when trying to explain its success. On the surface, the neoclassical perspective also seems like a natural view to take. Surely people prefer to get more for their money rather than less! And indeed, each time you spend money, you lose the opportunity to spend it on something else. And we all know that economic incentives matter, don't we?

However, some of the "natural flavor" is lost when these claims are sharpened, as neoclassical economics does: Do people really *always* prefer getting more rather than less – and even if they do, does this always affect how they behave? Are economic or other self-directed incentives really *all* that matters? And if so, exactly in what sense do people work like this? The position of mainstream economics is that people do to the extent that they are rational.

In this paper I discuss rationality as understood in neoclassical microeconomics by contrasting it with an anthropological interpretation of economic behavior, exemplified by recent work of Stephen Gudeman. Here a very different view of rational economizing is established. I side with this view in my critique of some aspects of the neoclassical understanding of rationality.

Before proceeding, I should underline that neoclassical economics includes a great number of models and theories, and a great number of positions. For almost any claim you feel tempted to make about neoclassical economics, there are a number of papers taking the opposite position. This is in fact an important aspect of how new pieces of work are generated: Assumptions in previous models are modified or removed in order to see what happens. What I discuss here is mainstream economics, that is, economics in its standard version – the standard equipment in the microeconomic toolbox, if you like. In some cases it is not all that clear what the standard version is, but basically it is what students get if they study economics at a university. Standard economics also plays a contrasting role when non-standard economic models are construed (Gibbard and Varian 1978; Hausman 1992;

Helgesson 2002; Klein 1998; Lind 1990, 1992; Sugden 2000).

The central assumptions in neoclassical microeconomics are presented in section 1. Institutional economics is briefly introduced in section 2 in order to underline certain aspects of mainstream economics, while section 3 accounts for Gudeman's approach to economic behavior. Section 4 contrasts neoclassical economic rationality with an anthropological view of rationality. This leads on to a discussion of two flaws of mainstream economics relating to rationality: its inability to distinguish between preferences and needs (section 5) and its inability to distinguish between preferences and values (section 6). The neoclassical conception of efficiency is discussed in section 7. Finally, my conclusions are summarized in section 8.

1. MAINSTREAM ECONOMICS

Microeconomics is generally described as the branch of economics that studies the decisions of individual households and firms and how individual markets work, while macroeconomics studies the economy as a whole and is concerned with large aggregates of behavior rather than with individual choices. So while microeconomics analyzes the behavior of particular consumers and firms and how their interactions affect resource allocation and income distribution, macroeconomics deals with aggregates such as total output, total employment, inflation, and the rate of economic growth, often on the national level (see, e.g., Lipsey and Chrystal 1995; Parkin 1994).

In mainstream microeconomics, consumers as well as producers are taken to be independent, self-interested, rational maximizers. As formulated by the economist Gary Becker, "the combined assumptions of maximizing behavior, market equilibrium, and stable preferences, used relentlessly and unflinchingly, form the heart of the economic approach" (Becker 1976:5). In a similar vein, the philosopher Daniel Hausman writes that "agents seeking their own material welfare is what makes economies run, and theories which dethrone this motive cease to be economics" (Hausman 1992:95).

The basic assumptions of the standard theory of consumer choice, which I will restrict myself to dealing with here, are *rationality*, *consumerism*, and *diminishing marginal rates of substitution*.

If every person is willing to exchange more of a commodity y for a unit of commodity x as the amount of y that she has increases relative to the amount of x that she has, then the condition of diminishing marginal rates of substitution is met. In other words, the more you have of some thing as compared to other things, the less the relative value of the last unit of that thing. I will say no more about this condition, since it is peripheral to my discussion.

According to the consumer choice theory, an agent is rational if and only if (a) her preferences are complete, transitive, and continuous and (b) she does not prefer any available (affordable) option to the one she chooses.

That preferences are *complete* means that the agent can compare all options. There will arise no situation where the alternatives cannot be ranked relative to one another. That preferences are *transitive* means that if you prefer alternative a to alternative b, and b to c, then you prefer a to c. Thus, if you prefer meat to fish, and fish to beans, then you prefer meat to beans if your preferences are transitive. That preferences are *continuous* means, roughly speaking, that small changes in prices lead to only small changes in demand. A curve showing your demand as related to various prices should not contain any sudden jumps (Hausman 1992:14–18, 30).[1]

Consumerism concerns the following three conditions: (a) the objects of the person's preferences are bundles of commodities consumed by the person herself, (b) there are no interdependencies between preferences of different persons, and (c) up to some usually unattained point individuals prefer larger commodity bundles to smaller.

It follows from the rationality assumptions that the agent maximizes, while consumerism brings in self-interest. When combined, these conditions state that rational economic agents maximize their own preference satisfaction, which in this context is to say that they maximize what they themselves get out of their consumption. In other words, neoclassical economics pictures people as choosing between fully comparable alternatives in a way that makes the outcome as good as it possibly can be for themselves (given their limited assets) while disregarding their families, colleagues, and friends, as well as

---

[1] On continuity, see also Varian (1999:521); cf. Mas-Colell et al. (1995:171).

the norms and expectations of the larger community, as far as their choices are concerned.[2]

That economists "picture" people in this way does not mean that they claim that people actually behave in this way (although sometimes they do).[3] What it means is that economists use models built on the assumption that people do, which is to say that they study what would be the case *if* people behaved in this way (Helgesson 2002, chap. 2 and pp. 175–177). Nevertheless, the understanding they get of how economies work rests on these assumptions, since this approach to economics is predominant.

2. INSTITUTIONAL ECONOMICS

The neoclassical understanding of economy is very different from that of, for instance, sociology, psychology, or anthropology. Considerable differences are found also in institutional economics, one of the few alternative frameworks in economics at present.[4] The latter seeks to ex-

[2] Unless the family is seen as the acting units – then choices are assumed to maximize what is good for the family. Feminists criticize this approach (as well) and argue that the use of the family as the smallest unit of analysis blocks insights into much of what goes on in real life; see, e.g., Nelson 1995:142–143.

[3] In economics textbooks it is fairly common to find claims that real economies are sufficiently like modeled economies for the conclusions of economic theory to be relevant to real events. Some examples are Kreps 1990:4–5; Mankiw 2001:154–157; and Parkin 1994:305.

[4] This succinct presentation is mainly based on Dugger 1994; Samuels 1991; and Söderbaum 2000.

plain human behavior by focusing on the institutional and cultural context rather than the autonomously acting individual. By institution is meant here "a set of norms and ideals which is imperfectly … reproduced or internalized through habituation" (Dugger 1994:338). The individual's choices are not seen as fundamental causal factors; instead, individual behavior is taken to be explained when it is shown to fit into an institutional structure of behavioral norms, which may be formal or informal. Norms, rules, rewards, sanctions, and power relations are factors of interest to the institutionalist, and they are all assumed to play a role for outcomes on markets.

Institutionalist economics maintains that the allocative mechanism at work "is not the pure conceptualized market *per se* but the institutions, or power structure, which form and operate through the actual market" (Samuels 1991:106). Thus, institutionalists have a broader conception of economies and economics than neoclassical economics does, since institutionalists include the factors that shape the actual economies, while neoclassical economics restricts itself to analyzing what happens in these (or more abstract) markets. Among the factors considered by institutional economics are institutions such as those of property, contract, and legal rights.

Compared to mainstream economists, who strongly prefer simplicity, institutionalists are more interested in realism and the details of particular cases: "Occam's razor, in neoclassical hands, is used to cut away all the messy details (which institutionalists crave and neoclassicists abhor)" (Dugger 1994:339). Institutionalists conduct case studies and have quite a lot in common with anthropologists, both in terms of method and by being sensitive to evaluative and ideological issues, while neoclassical economists are fonder of abstract analysis and theoretical modeling. In their critique of neoclassical economics, institutionalists protest particularly strongly against the "mechanistic application of rationality, competition, knowledge, and *inter alia*, methodological individualism" (Samuels 1991:107).

3. AN ANTHROPOLOGICAL VIEW OF ECONOMY

Stephen Gudeman has studied different aspects of economy from an anthropological perspective since the 1960s. His many examples in *The Anthropology of Economy* show that there is a considerable variation in economic practices – far greater than what is reflected in economics textbooks and in neoclassical research.

Gudeman argues that economy, across cultures, consists of two realms, market and community. "Both facets make up economy," he writes, "for humans are motivated by social fulfillment, curiosity, and the pleasure of mastery, as well as instrumental purpose, competition, and the accumulation of gains." "Community" is here understood as concrete, "on-the-ground" associations as well as more abstract solidarities, while "market" refers to anonymous, instrumental exchanges "abstracted from social context" (Gudeman 2001:1).

Gudeman discusses the two realms of economy in terms of the "up-close" and the "far-distant." From the far-distant perspective, economy is impersonal, leaving social context irrelevant: here socially separated, inde-

pendent agents interact, each motivated by her own expected benefits from trade. From the up-close perspective, economy is local, specific, and constituted through
social relationships and contextually defined values. The
individual is "embedded" in a web of dependencies, obligations, common plans, and creation of meaning, far from
the independent, isolated unit pictured in neoclassical
economics.

There is a complex relationship between the two
realms. Even when people do business in an impersonal,
calculated way their activities are dependent on "the presence of communal relations and resources for [their] success." The community realm is the cultural and institutional context in which these market activities take place
and on which their existence depends (Gudeman 2001:1–
2, 11–12; quote from p. 2).

That there is such a community background even to
rational market transactions may seem utterly trivial to
anthropologists. However, this fact is mainly ignored in
neoclassical economics. There you can still make sense of
the idea of a "self-made man," even though we all know
that this man was born of a woman, protected, nourished,
encultured, and educated for many years, and when he
grew older and, in his social sphere, got some fruitful ideas,
was able to use various financing institutions to get the
money to get his business started and society's entire web
of services and communications to keep it running, which
eventually might give him the confidence to claim that
he was all self-made. This view of economic agents has
made feminists argue that neoclassical economics deals
with a "mushroom man" – that is, an agent suddenly

sprung to full maturity like a mushroom. It exaggerates the individual's independence, as if her actions take place outside a social context, hides the effects of the individual's background and history on what she accomplishes as an adult, and disregards dependencies and power-relations between individuals, for instance between men and women and between parents and their children in different stages of life (cf. Nelson 1995).

While the far-distant realm concerns activities whose meaning comes from their instrumental value, economic activities in the up-close realm become valuable also in themselves: "The market realm revolves about short-term material relationships that are undertaken *for the sake of* achieving a project or securing a good. In the communal realm, material goods are exchanged through relationships kept *for their own sake*," for example, as gifts (Gudeman 2001:8, 10, 36; cf. Anderson 1993). Family and friendship relations are examples of such relations valued for their own sake.

Gudeman reminds us that economic activity is not limited to situations in which commodities, food and drink, for instance, are *bought* – to store and cook the food are also economic activities, and so is sharing at the table. In kind they are, of course, very different from, say, buying or selling stock over the Internet, since they involve close social relationships and commitments. Commitments and social values in connection to economic activities undeniably play a role also outside the household sphere: sometimes among neighbors, at the village level, in teams, and among colleagues, to give but a few examples.

From this rough categorization of an anthropological view of economy it may be argued that mainstream economics covers economy as far-distant, while the up-close perspective is what anthropology adds to the standard economic perspective. There is something to this, although this description is not entirely correct. On the anthropological account, both realms are realms in the real world. In neoclassical economics, market analyses concern a mechanism maintained by the "market forces" rather than concrete markets – the market is here a strongly idealized entity of importance to economic modeling, and the question of whether there is a correspondence between model and reality is often not even addressed (Helgesson 2002; cf. Hausman 1992; Lind 1990).

4. IRRATIONAL BEHAVIOR OR OVERSIMPLIFIED EXPLANATION?

Gudeman gives many examples of economic activities that seem to need another explanatory basis than the one offered by standard economics, basically because they do not consist, or do not consist exclusively, of exchanges between maximizing agents on a market. One fascinating example is the *dzamalag* ceremony among the Gunwinggu in Northern Australia, where trade between different groups consists of goods such as cloth, blankets, and spears.

> Soon, two visiting men began to sing while a third played a pipe. Their music initiated *dzamalag*. Initially, two Gunwinggu women … presented each [of the singing men] with a piece of cloth; they hit and touched the men and uttered erotic jokes. … Shortly,

another Gunwinggu woman ... did the same with [the pipe player]. Then, other Gunwinggu women arose, and selecting a visiting man ..., gave him cloth, struck him lightly, and invited him to have sexual relations. The pairs retired and copulated, after which the visiting men gave the Gunwinggu women tobacco and beads. Returning to the dancing ground, the Gunwinggu women gave the tobacco and beads to their Gunwinggu spouses. Gunwinggu men then arose, and each gave a blanket to a visiting woman. ... Striking her lightly and inviting her to copulate, the two retired to the bushes, after which the male offered his partner tobacco and beads, and she shared them with her spouse. Finally, Gunwinggu women lined up in two rows. The visiting men, brandishing their spears, danced toward them saying, "We will not spear you, for we have already speared you with our penes". They gave the spears to the women, and a large food distribution was held which completed *dzamalag*. (Gudeman 2001:124–125)

Even though it could be argued that the participants in this ceremony are engaged in self-interested maximizing behavior (exclusively directed at facilitating trade), this seems like a far-fetched or at least very incomplete explanation. It is reasonable to explain their behavior in terms of its inherent social meaning in that community. Here trade is one aspect, another is the ritualized display of non-aggression, and a third is the expansion of community to include both the visiting and the visited group. The main point is that trade was not the only reason for coming together (alternatively, trade meant more than exchanging goods).

Another example Gudeman gives is the tradition of household groups among the Iban of Sarawak to treat a certain strain of rice as sacred and to expend great effort on reproducing it, while not paying similar attention to the rest of the rice field. The sacred strain of rice is its *padi pun* and is never traded or even lent to others, while these restrictions do not apply to the rest of the rice harvest. The *padi pun* stands for the identity and power of the household (Gudeman 2001:32–33).

This expression of identity-making does not make much sense from a neoclassical perspective. The essence of the neoclassical market view is that everything is for sale at the right price; what does not fit that description cannot be understood. Such an approach can hardly be reconciled with the behavior described here, unless it is re-described in a way that leaves out some of its central features.

Economic rationality in its neoclassical version has difficulties making sense even of certain aspects of ordinary Western market behavior. For example, consider trust. Trust is a prerequisite for well-functioning markets. While contracts, property rights, and commercial law are all needed in modern market-oriented economic systems, transaction costs will be substantially lower if these institutions are supplemented by trust. In its absence, market participants will need a number of costly precautions in order not to be cheated, such as highly specified contracts (Fukuyama 1995; Hollis 1998; Putnam et al 1992).[5]

[5] Maybe one should include in this ethical base needed for smooth communication and exchange, not only trust but also honesty, mutuality, cooperativeness, benevolence, a feeling of responsibility, caring, and respect (cf. Gudeman 2001:18).

Although trust is of great importance to the efficiency of markets, it is hard to grasp within a neoclassical framework. The problem is that neoclassical economics defines rationality in terms of the agent's expected utility, "whereas trust requires that we can expect people to ignore this siren call" (Hollis 1998:79).

It is not only difficult for such an agent to be trustworthy. It is also difficult to find such a person really trusting. A rational agent may try to calculate whether it would be worthwhile to trust someone or not, considering possible gains and losses and their estimated probabilities, but it is something completely different to go from there to actually trusting the person. Trust has little to do with rational calculation of this kind – trusting someone means finding it unnecessary to calculate the risk of being failed. Indeed, people rely on others long before they have the capacity to do any self-centered calculations, even before they have any definite sense of self. In the Gunwinggu example, cited above, a ceremony takes place to express that the two groups can trust each other. However, that they already do is a prerequisite for the ceremony to take place as described.

Trust presupposes community. Community, in turn, presupposes shared values and norms, such as that of promise-keeping (e.g., Fukuyama 1995:10; Hollis 1998:22). The problem for community with self-directed rational maximizers is that they do what they promise to do only if they would do it anyway. To cooperate with such people is risky and may not be worthwhile, since they will break the deal as soon as an alternative gives a higher pay-off, no matter how small the difference. It goes without saying that such behavior is harmful to business relations. The expected utility of cooperation is normally much greater if one's business partners can be relied on.

Maximizing behavior is a problem even to the rational maximizers themselves, since they will not be able to reach the optimal outcome for themselves in choice situations involving other rational maximizers. This point is illustrated by the "Prisoner's Dilemma," which describes a choice situation in which two prisoners, each making an isolated, rational choice based on what is best for him, end up with an outcome far worse than what would have resulted from a more communitarian choice strategy (see, e.g., Hollis 1998: 68–69).

A thoroughly instrumental attitude towards social relations not only threatens business relations but constitutes a general threat to deep relations between individuals, and in the extension, to the bonds and ties of society. One may therefore argue that neoclassical thinking on rationality works against trust, since it moves attention from community to individual goals and makes the economic agent think of others exclusively as means to her own fulfillment and not as other individuals to respect and value for their own sake (cf. Gudeman 2001:137–140; Anderson 1993). Such an attitude also reduces activities valued for their own sake to activities as means, thereby changing the perspective on many of the things people do, turning activities into something done for instrumental reasons only, rather than, as before, also for being meaningful in themselves (cf., e.g., Gudeman 2001:130–131).[6]

Gudeman sketches another, complementary view of rationality, what he calls "situated reason," which concerns know-how and practical problem-solving for the maintenance of communal life. More specifically, it concerns the protection of a social and resource base, improvements of things and tools through adjustments and inventions, finding ways to handle everyday problems in a more convenient way, and thereby increasing security (assurance against uncertainty) and well-being. Examples given are knowledge and development of ways to harvest potatoes, pick maize, cook food, and farm. Coping by adaptation, adjustment, and step-by-step improvement is stressed as an important aspect of this kind of rationality. Gudeman claims that situated reason is always an important part of economy:

> Rational decision-making presumes an ordered world in the sense that items or units exist and are commensurate. Situated reason makes a world, and opens new worlds, dissolving oppositions between self and others, self and objects. It is part of economy at the base. (Gudeman 2001:38–42; quote from p. 42)

Although in need of being worked out in greater detail, an important point underlined by this view of rationality, and missed in neoclassical economics, is the need of a rationality concept that naturally connects to everyday practicality.

[6] See also his discussion of sacra and economy at the base, chap. 2.

Further, rationality in this sense reaches beyond the individual's own interests. People belong to a number of communities – families, neighborhoods, businesses, networks, and nations – against whose interests they balance their own private interests. In doing so, they do not lose their rationality but rather show an awareness of their connectedness to others. By cooperating, trusting, and being trustworthy they come to live richer lives and may even reach outcomes that are out of reach for the narrowly maximizing agent.[7]

An aspect of situated reason is the special attitude towards self-sufficiency that is found in several farming societies, and elsewhere. In many communities a clear distinction is made, both in principle and in practice, between production for sustenance and production for gain, reflecting the difference in importance between making a living and making a profit. The basic crop may be given a special, sometimes sacred, status. Rather than simply being a means of survival, these products then become symbols of identity and are regarded as intrinsically valuable. For instance, for the Kelabit in Sarawak, rice is both the central food and an item of symbolic importance. Failure to produce enough of it leads to dependence on others and loss of self-esteem. For the Kekchi Maya of southern Belize, corn is a necessity and the central food – a part of every meal and offered at house altars (Gudeman 2001:36–38, 43–48). According to Gudeman, self-sufficiency "helps create and maintain the commons, and

---

[7] Cf. the Prisoner's Dilemma. Also cf. Hollis 1998; Kramer et al. 1996.

45

marks independence and the borders of a group" (ibid.:43).

5. PREFERENCES AND NEEDS

In contrast to the attitude expressed in the examples above, mainstream economics does not distinguish between economic activities concerning subsistence and economic activities concerning what lies beyond that. That is, neoclassical economics does not distinguish between preferences concerning needs and preferences concerning other things. Consequentially, in mainstream economics needs are treated no differently than other preferences.

This is peculiar, since people's well-being at least partly depends on the degree to which their needs are satisfied. A person may need something even though she has no preference for it and not getting it may be harmful to her, as would be the case if someone with severe diabetes did not get insulin. In the ordinary walk of life, needs are necessarily connected to well-being, while the connection between any possible preference and well-being is not similarly granted.[8] There are preferences the satisfaction of which makes no difference at all to one's well-being, and the satisfaction of some preferences may do more harm than good. As Daniel Hausman and Michael Pherson laconically remark, "[I]t takes no great philosoph-

[8] I write "in the ordinary walk of life" since attending a person's bodily needs towards the end of her life may not enhance her well-being. However, to the extent that getting on with one's life is a central prerequisite for well-being, then needs are connected to well-being.

ical talent to recognize that giving a powerful motorcycle to a reckless teenage boy does not necessarily make him better off, no matter how desperately he wants it" (Helgesson 2002:181–182).[9]

It may, of course, be the case that a rational person *has* preferences concerning her needs, but it does not follow from the neoclassical definition of economic rationality that a rational person cares about her needs. Economic rationality concerns the realization of ends, not the choice of ends; that is, in neoclassical terminology, it concerns the satisfaction of preferences, not what preferences to have. This goes against the common-sense view of rationality: There *may* be instances where it is not irrational to disregard one's needs, but if there are, they are exceptional cases.[10]

To most non-economists it is clear both that people may not prefer that which would be most conducive to their well-being and that they may ignore their needs. Sometimes people just don't care about their long-term interests, sometimes they misjudge their alternatives, and sometimes out of ignorance they never consider the alternative that would be most conducive to their well-being. There may also be special reasons why certain preferences are not formed. For example, certain preferences may be psychologically blocked since the hardships of life would be even worse to bear if one often got disappointed. Thus, there may be many things that a poor per-

---

[9] The quote is from Hausman and McPherson (1996:73).

[10] See Gudeman (2001:56–57), for examples of community apportionment to assure that needs are satisfied.

son does not have any actual preferences for since she finds it so utterly unrealistic that such preferences would ever be satisfied. As the economist Amartya Sen puts it, "[T]he hopelessly deprived lack the courage to desire much" (Sen 1987:45–47, quote p. 46; Elster 1982).[11]

Economists sometimes use a rather odd argument for limiting welfare discussions to preference satisfaction, and that is that it would be paternalistic to claim that there are things that are good for people even if they do not want them – for instance, that it is good for anorectic persons to eat even if they do not want to. Even if it were paternalistic to make such claims, which it is not, it could still be the case that some things *are* good for people whether they like it or not. To me it is obvious that there are such things. To agree with this is to agree that there are generally shared needs and that they owe their special status to the fact that they are particularly important for people to attend to regardless of whether they are important *according to* people (Helgesson 2002:189).[12]

One might suspect that value-subjectivism lurks behind the inability of economic theory to distinguish needs from other preferences. If this is the case, it means that the inability to distinguish between "preferences" and "needs" depends on the inability to distinguish between "preferences" and "values."

[11] Elster calls the latter phenomenon "adaptive preference formation."

[12] On paternalism, see Arneson (1998).

6. PREFERENCES AND VALUES

Mainstream economics does not seem capable of making sense of the difference between *preferences* and *values* – instead it places everything that the agent cares for in a single category, whether it concerns her preference for green olives over black ones or for a moment's silence on the bus, or her view on abortion or the death penalty. In neoclassical economics, deeply rooted values are just preferences among other preferences. This approach excludes the possibility of objective values, or re-dresses them beyond recognition. From the individual's point of view, the neoclassical treatment of preferences means a leveling out of differences between whimsical wishes, desires, goals, plans, dreams, principles, ideals, and profound rules of conduct.

An important idea in the neoclassical analysis of economic behavior is that people reveal their preferences through their choices on the market. The basic idea is that the more you want something, the more you are willing to pay for it, which will be reflected in your behavior.

But our willingness to pay is affected not only by the (relative) strength of our preferences and our ability to pay. There are things that we are not willing to pay for even though we value them highly – this may be because we think that they should not be handled on the market. For instance, many Swedes would be unwilling to pay for taking a walk in the woods or swimming in the lakes because they think you should have the right to do this without paying (cf. Anderson 1993, chap. 9).

Putting a price tag on certain things may even be seen

as diminishing their value – some things may be so valuable that they are priceless. For that reason some people would be unwilling to put a price tag on the value, for instance, of certain untouched landscapes. Or take an example referred to by Gudeman: A U.S. citizen is upset that the American flag is for sale and gives the following explanation: "If the flag is really precious, why do we sell it at K-Mart ... when it was sold, that's when it lost its meaning" (Gudeman 2001:49, note 6). Here is another example: John gladly pays for a new car, but he would never consider paying to get Lisa for his wife, yet he cares much more for her than for the car.

Some things are what they are only if they are freely given and not bought and sold, such as love and friendship. These things are completely different from consumer goods, since they cannot be given their proper meaning in a market context. Maybe part of the reason is that as far as they exist, they are mutually constituted and thereby depend on more than the instrumental use-value from the perspective of a single agent. For instance, a gift may symbolize special bonds between giver and receiver; if this relation changes, so does the meaning of that gift – one might say that the gift changes from carrying all those meanings that were loaded into it to meaning something else, perhaps much less.

Some of the things one comes to think of here are held sacred in the community. They do not belong in the market place because they may not be sold – they have a central role as marks of identity, and selling them would in a sense mean to sell the community. Examples are the

British Crown Jewels and the U.S. Constitution in Washington, D.C. (Gudeman 2001:28–32).

Gudeman presents another reason why we may be unwilling to put price-tags on, for example, "environmental assets": "To place a price on a forest, a river, the air, or a lake implies its future value is determinant and not subject to repositioning." But the potential value and uses of our environment "must be addressed in the light of economy's many values, for we cannot predict the meanings and uses" that it may have in the future (Gudeman 2001:156–157).

You may also disapprove of there being certain things for sale on the market because you think such things should not exist, like prostitution, pornography, arms, and drugs. How can you express this on the market? Your disapproval of the fact that certain things are *not* for sale on the market is equally difficult to express on the market.[13]

Some of the preferences that cannot be expressed on markets are *about* markets and their conditions, others are about other social institutions, how they should be organized, and so on. For example, some preferences may concern the idea that certain things should not be handled on the market but by democratically controlled institutions. People may see a value in democratic decision-

---

[13] What product should you buy in your grocery store in order to express that you are disappointed that they no longer offer your favorite cheese for sale – a postcard saying "Damn you!"? It may, of course, be used to *tell them* that you are disappointed. Anderson (1993, chap. 7) argues that markets leave no room for voice, only for exit.

making – to value such decision-procedures is something very different from being willing to pay for them. One reason to think that some things should not be handled on the market is that some matters are common interests. In such cases there may be a point in not immediately casting a vote, by expressing one's willingness to pay for various alternatives and rather listening to the reasons people have for having the preferences they have and publicly debating the pros and cons of the alternatives at hand. By testing different arguments for and against, people may not only express their views but also change their minds. The market is certainly not the best forum for debate and reconsideration, nor are we represented by an equal vote (cf. Anderson 1993, esp. pp. 158–167; Sagoff 1988).

By moving common matters to the market arena, community is weakened or diminished—what was once common ground transforms into assets that individuals compete for. Gudeman argues that "when capital expands, we often find the debasement of community as its values evaporate in support of the market" (Gudeman 2001:22 [which includes the quote], 163).[14] He therefore sees economy as "built on the tension between making rational calculations and maintaining connections with others" (Gudeman 2001:149).

---

[14] See further, pp. 27–28: "The so-called 'tragedy of the commons', which refers to destruction of a resource through unlimited use by individuals, is a tragedy not of a physical commons but of a human community, because of the failure of its members to treat one another as communicants and its transformation to a competitive situation."

7. RATIONALITY AS EFFICIENCY

Although building on assumptions whose realism and relevance must be questioned, mainstream economics is used for practical purposes in many areas, and it is commonly held to have important things to say about efficiency and thus about economizing.

Economic efficiency, like rationality, is tied to maximization, although maximization of a special kind. According to the central notion of efficiency, *Pareto efficiency*, an economy is Pareto efficient if and only if it is impossible to make someone better off, by changing the allocation, without making someone else worse off. If an allocation is Pareto efficient, then there is no available alternative in which some individual is better off and no other individual is worse off. An allocation is inefficient if such an improvement can take place. Pareto efficiency concerns well-being. As we have seen, in mainstream economics this is understood in terms of preference satisfaction (cf. Sen 1987; Varian 1999).

> The 'fundamental' Pareto finding about efficient markets has been so influential among economists and in the popular wisdom that today economic rationality means efficiency. … Efficiency has become the supreme value in market economy. (Gudeman 2001:96)

There is much to say in favor of being efficient and for using resources efficiently, as long as this is understood in a sense that regards all the relevant aspects. For example, it seems important to get as much as possible out of our common resources for health care. This may, for instance, motivate economic analyses of cost-effectiveness. However, this is something altogether different from using the Pareto criterion in welfare analyses, and there is much to say against the welfare relevance of Pareto efficiency, which should be clear from what has been said in the two previous sections. There we saw that the preference-based approach fails to distinguish between preferences and needs and between preferences and values. To the list of criticism one may add mainstream economics' treatment of interpersonal comparisons and willingness to pay.

The neoclassical notion of Pareto efficiency excludes interpersonal comparisons of well-being. For any comparison between two alternative states of affairs where some people are better off and some people are worse off in one of the states compared to the other, the Pareto criterion has nothing to say about what allocation is the more efficient one. This incomparability is absolute. As is easily seen, this has absurd consequences. Thus, an allocation, A, cannot be said to be either better or worse than another allocation, B, even if millions of people are much better off in A (the difference may be that between severe poverty and comfortable middle-class lives) while a single well-off person is slightly worse off in A than in B. It goes without saying that redistribution will appear to be an uninteresting policy tool from such a perspective.

Admittedly, interpersonal comparisons of well-being may sometimes be hard to verify, but by excluding them much is lost. Since benefits and harms usually fall on different individuals in different policy alternatives, interpersonal welfare comparisons are needed unless we are to abstain from most of the policy evaluations that are made today. As it stands, the Pareto criterion is extremely weak as an evaluative tool. To save the day, economists have therefore introduced the notion of *potential* Pareto improvements. An alternative is a potential Pareto improvement if those who would gain from having that alternative realized would be better off even if they compensated the potential losers up to a point where no one would be worse off in that alternative. It is a potential Pareto improvement because it would be an actual Pareto improvement if the compensations were actually paid. However, it does not matter to the idea of potential Pareto improvements whether compensations are actually paid or not.

Critics have pointed out that if no compensation is paid, then some people will be worse off than before. Further, the fact that the gainers could compensate the losers does not necessarily mean that the welfare losses are smaller than the welfare gains – they may be greater. On the other hand, if compensations are paid, then the alternative is not only a potential Pareto improvement but also an actual Pareto improvement. Therefore the idea of potential Pareto improvements has little to contribute, apart from drawing attention to the option of using compensation to gain acceptance from potential losers (cf. Hausman and McPherson 1996:93ff.).

In ordinary life we do make interpersonal comparisons of well-being. Certainly we know who is better off, the man who got his leg crushed in a political riot or the man next to him who did not get hurt. And we quite often know if some resources would be of greater help to one person than to another. As the economist Roy Harrod put it in the 1930s, "[W]e cannot decide with certainty whether two pence have more utility to a millionaire or a beggar. Yet we have a shrewd suspicion" (Harrod 1938:396). It is hard to see how economic efficiency claims can be of more than marginal relevance if interpersonal comparisons of well-being are excluded, or replaced by the potential willingness to pay for a certain outcome.

As I noted in the previous section, the neoclassical analysis of economic behavior assumes that people reveal their preferences through their choices on the market. One idea is that the strength of a person's preferences is reflected in her willingness to pay. Some reasons against accepting such a simple connection between preferences and behavior were discussed, the main point being that there are some things we value highly even though we are not willing to pay for them. However, there are reasons why there is no straightforward connection between preferences and willingness to pay that, from an economic perspective, may seem more basic. The most obvious one is that it does not follow from the fact that a person has no ability to pay, that the person has no preferences.

Secondly, although a person's willingness to pay normally says something about her preferences – the more she wants some good the more she is likely to be willing to pay for it – a similar conclusion cannot be drawn from different people's willingness to pay. A rich man and a poor man may both want to buy a house, but the rich man can afford to pay more. This does not show that he has the stronger preference for it. Even if the poor man could pay the amount that the rich man is willing to pay, the poor man would then have to make greater sacrifices in terms of other things that he wants. Therefore, to be willing to pay the same amount for the house as the rich man, the poor man would have to have a stronger preference for it. Generally, projects that benefit the rich will be favored and those that benefit the poor will be disfavored if one evaluates public projects in terms of the total willingness to pay. Basically this is so since the rich can be expected to be willing to pay more than the poor for the same thing. This, in turn, depends on the differences in their abilities to pay. This also means that even if the total willingness to pay for some project A is higher than the total willingness to pay for project B, it is still an open question what project is most valuable in the sense of being most beneficial to those concerned in terms of well-being.

From the neoclassical perspective, transactions based on community values represent irrationalities, frictions, or externalities to an otherwise efficient system (Gudeman 2001:6). Gudeman notes that "economists argue that the transaction costs of managing a communal distribution are high, but these costs are nothing other than the maintenance of social relationships or mutuality itself" (Gudeman 2001:64). In other words, discussions focused on the efficiency costs caused by redistribution, for instance via taxes and various welfare programs, tend to hide the fact that what is at stake is what kind of society we want. The application of the Pareto criterion may in fact contribute to an ideological redirection.

> Arguments about community apportionment today are posed often as a trade-off between efficiency and equity. ... But community equity ... cannot be 'traded' for market efficiency, because they pertain to different realms of value. The 'trade-off' concerns the relative place of community and market values in an economy. (Gudeman 2001:65)

In order to find an efficient solution to a choice situation that we are facing we must first identify what is important in the situation at hand. If we fail to do this then there is little hope that the solutions we come up with will be any good. Thus, in order to be able to make priorities in accordance with our values we must keep clear exactly what components we are dealing with in the efficiency-equity dichotomy. It is by no means obvious that efficiency according to some standard is more important than the community values that may be defended and supported by applying some form of apportionment of resources. Further, as has been argued above, there is reason to question the relevance of the notion of Pareto efficiency used in mainstream economics.

8. CONCLUDING REMARKS

An essential feature of mainstream economics is its conception of rationality, which connects self-directed maximizing behavior and preference satisfaction. In this paper I have questioned the reasonableness of treating rationality in this way by arguing that there is no direct link between preference satisfaction and well-being. The main objections have been that mainstream economics fails to distinguish between preferences and needs and between preferences and values and thereby fails to grasp central facets of human life. Nor can its calculations on efficiency be accepted in more than, at most, a restricted number of cases. Another point that has been made is that trust, which is of great importance to human interaction in business and elsewhere, is a blind spot for neoclassical economics.

One of the most important contributions an anthropological perspective on economy can make, I think, is to remind us of what we already know, or have an inkling of, but tend to forget under the influence of the neoclassical understanding of economic activity. Much, although far from all, of what is systematically and intentionally ignored in the neoclassical analysis is relevant to how economies work. By leaving it aside, neoclassical economics leaves important aspects of real-life economies aside. Simplicity has always been a guiding light in neoclassical economics, and much has been gained that way, but the longer such an approach is pursued the higher the costs will be – eventually one will have an extremely systematic understanding of a limited number of aspects of that which one once set out to make sense of. An anthropological approach to economy can counteract this development by bringing out the complexities of our economic realities and reminding us of the distortions caused by viewing economies through the lens of neoclassical economic theory.

REFERENCES

Anderson, Elizabeth. 1993. *Value in Ethics and Economics*. Cambridge, Mass.: Harvard University Press.

Arneson, Richard J. 1998. "Paternalism," *Routledge Encyclopedia of Philosophy*, vol. 7, ed. Edward Craig, pp. 250–525. London: Routledge.

Becker, Gary. 1976. *The Economic Approach to Human Behavior*. Chicago: University of Chicago Press.

Dugger, William, 1994. "Methodological Differences between Institutional and Neoclassical Economics," *The Philosophy of Economics*, 2nd ed., ed. Daniel Hausman, pp. 336–345. Cambridge: Cambridge University Press.

Elster, Jon. 1982. "Sour Grapes – Utilitarianism and the Genesis of Wants," *Utilitarianism and Beyond*, ed. Amartya Sen and Bernard Williams, pp. 219–238. Cambridge: Cambridge University Press.

Fukuyama, Francis. 1995. *Trust: The Social Virtues and the Creation of Prosperity*. New York: Free Press.

George, Susan, and Fabrizio Sabelli. 1994. *Faith and Credit: The World Bank's Secular Empire*. Harmonsworth: Penguin Books.

Gibbard, Allan, and Hal R. Varian. 1978. "Economic Models," *The Journal of Philosophy*, vol. 75, pp. 664–677.

Gudeman, Stephen. 2001. *The Anthropology of Economy. Community, Market, and Culture*. Oxford: Blackwell Publishing.

Harrod, Roy F. 1938. "Scope and Method of Economics," *Economic Journal*, vol. 38, pp. 383–412.

Hausman, Daniel. 1992. *The Inexact and Separate Science of Economics*. Cambridge: Cambridge University Press.

Hausman, Daniel, and Michael McPherson. 1996. *Economic Analysis and Moral Philosophy*. Cambridge: Cambridge University Press.

Helgesson, Gert. 2002. *Values, Norms & Ideology in Mainstream Economics*, Diss. Uppsala University.

Hollis, Martin. 1998. *Trust within Reason*. Cambridge: Cambridge University Press.

Klein, Erwin. 1998. *Economic Theories and their Relational Structures*. Basingstoke: Macmillan Press.

Kramer, Roderick M., Marilynn B. Brewer and Benjamin A. Hanna. 1996. "Collective Trust and Collective Action: The Decision to Trust as a Social Decision," *Trust in Organizations: Frontiers of Theory and Research*, ed. Roderick M. Kramer and Tom R. Tyler, pp. 357–389. Thousand Oaks: Sage Publications.

Kreps, David M. 1990. *A Course in Microeconomic Theory*. New York: Harvester Wheatsheaf.

Lind, Hans. 1990. *Tanken bakom tänkta ekonomier: Om forskningsstrategi i modern nationalekonomi. [The Image behind Imagined Economies: On Research Strategy in Modern Economics]* Stockholm: Akademeja.

—. 1992. "A Case Study of Normal Research in Theoretical Economics," *Economics and Philosophy*, vol. 8, pp. 83–102.

Lipsey, Richard G., and K. Alex Chrystal. 1995. *An Introduction to Positive Economics*, 8th ed. Oxford: Oxford University Press.

Mankiw, N. Gregory. 2001. *Principles of Economics*, 2nd ed. Fort Worth: Harcourt College Publishers.

Mas-Colell, Andreu, Michael D. Whinston and Jerry R. Green. 1995. *Microeconomic Theory*. Oxford: Oxford University Press.

Nelson, Julie A. 1995. "Feminism and Economics," *Journal of Economic Perspectives*, vol. 9, pp. 131–148.

Parkin, Michael. 1994. *Economics*, 2nd ed. Reading, Mass.:Addison-Wesley Publishing Company.

Putnam, Robert D. with Robert Leonardi and Raffaella Y. Nanetti. 1992. *Making Democracy Work: Civic Traditions in Modern Italy*. Princeton: Princeton University Press.

Sagoff, Mark. 1988. *The Economy of the Earth*. Cambridge: Cambridge University Press.

Samuels, Warren J. 1991. "Institutional Economics," *Companion to Contemporary Economic Thought*, ed. David Greenaway, Michael Bleaney and Ian Stewart, pp. 105–118. London: Routledge.

Sen, Amartya. 1987. *On Ethics and Economics*. Oxford: Blackwell.

Sugden, Robert. 2000. "Credible Worlds: The Status of Theoretical Models in Economics," *Journal of Economic Methodology*, vol. 7, pp. 1–31.

Söderbaum, Peter. 2000. *Ecological Economics: A Political Economics Approach to Environment and Development.* London: Earthscan.

Varian, Hal R. 1999. *Intermediate Economics: A Modern Approach,* 5th ed. New York: W.W. Norton.

RESISTING THE BLACK HOLE OF NEOCLASSICAL FORMALISM IN ECONOMIC ANTHROPOLOGY

A POLEMIC

ALF HORNBORG

Over the years, I have found much of Stephen Gudeman's work very useful as a means of relativizing (or "defamiliarizing"[1]) standard categories of economics. In particular, his book *Economics as Culture: Models and Metaphors of Livelihood* (1986) showed how different categories of people in various historical and geographical contexts – ethnographically documented Africans and Melanesians as well as nineteenth century British economists and their modern descendants – have conceptualized exchange and material provisioning in radically different but ubiquitously *cultural* ways. To any science founded – like economics – on the authority of its privileged perspective, this should be a powerfully subversive mes-

---

[1] The useful notion of "defamiliarization" was introduced by George E. Marcus and Michael M. J. Fischer, 1986.

sage. Admittedly, Gudeman did make a distinction between local/metaphorical models and universal/deriva-
tional/mathematical (i.e., Western) models,[2] but his point
was finally to transcend this distinction by showing that
universal models are "another set of local formulations"
(ibid.:viii), the special rationale of which is the aspira-
tion to subsume and eclipse other local models (ibid.:154–
157). "Imperialism," Gudeman concluded, may be re-
thought of in terms of "who gets to model whom." To me,
this conclusion suggests a final, reflexive victory of substantivism over formalism in economic anthropology,
applying cultural relativism so as to expose and challenge
the political agenda of master narratives in economics. It
represents the postmodernist turn in anthropology at its
best, while it still has something serious and politically
subversive to say.

To say that something is "cultural" is usually understood as a way of *relativizing* it, by showing to what extent it is arbitrarily "constructed," as the idiom goes. This
is a project that I have understood to be the main thrust
of Gudeman's work for decades. Against this background,
I must admit that reading his recent *The Anthropology of
Economy: Community, Market, and Culture* (2001) was
somewhat disappointing. To maintain the existence of a
universal duality of "market" versus "community" in all
societies seems like an unnecessary concession to formalist discourse. Though this generalization was apparently

[2] Gudeman occasionally uses "logical" or "rational" as synonyms
for the latter, but then concedes that local models can also be
logical and rational.

64

intended as a challenge to neoclassical theory, I imagine that formalists will be more content with finding market principles posited as universal (albeit in different proportions and applications) than they will be prompted to argue against the ubiquity of its counterpoint, i.e., "community" or "base" – particularly when the latter is defined diffusely enough to be able to encompass everything that is judged as somehow fundamental to society, including, it seems, the constitutional support of market enterprise (Gudeman 2001:29).

Whether intentionally or not, this book is more entrenched in conventional economic discourse than Gudeman's defamiliarizing stance in *Economics as Culture* fifteen years earlier. In his continuing conversations with economists since then, Gudeman seems increasingly to have gravitated (back) toward their contagious vocabulary, which he admits to having imbibed as a student. Substantial sections of *The Anthropology of Economy* read more like a textbook in economics than a contribution to anthropology.[3] It is easy to appreciate how much smoother such conversations with economists will be the more they are conducted in "their" terms – and how much less subversive. Instead of exposing – as in his earlier work – what Raymond Williams and, more recently, David Harvey (1996) have called "the politics of abstraction," Gude-

---

[3] Just to give an example, the discussion of "profit" on page 104 leaves me wondering what happened to the "anthropology" in "economic anthropology": "Normal profit is the return secured for innovations made in conditions of uncertainty.... A perfect market efficiently reallocates input uses and products through the price system."

man now seems to be content with pursuing new abstractions (e.g., "community," "base") to complement those of the economists. The crucial concerns with the very epistemology of exchange seem to have been jettisoned in his determination to develop a "comparative economic anthropology" (Gudeman 2001:4–5). In declaring that *Economics as Culture* did not qualify as "comparative economic anthropology," he reveals that his conception of such a project is in fact fundamentally formalist. In the present volume, he is finally able to pursue this task by framing human life everywhere in terms of a very limited set of abstract categories.

Gudeman's sympathetic championing of *community* – as the ubiquitous counterpoint to *market* – is sadly undermined by the vagueness of its definition. The analytical polarity on which his argument is founded soon dissolves into contradictions. At the outset, community is defined as the up-close/local/specific/contextual and market as the far-distant/impersonal/abstracted from context (ibid.:1). But even here, on the first page, the distinction is muddled by the inclusion, in community, of "imagined solidarities that people experience," as if imagined solidarities could not be impersonal and abstract. This latter objection is in fact validated already on page 9, where Gudeman observes that communities "may be small as well as ethnic groups or states held together by force and ideologies," and further on, when he states that they may include "imagined groupings that never meet," such as owners of Apple computers (ibid.:25), global charities (ibid.:26), and perhaps even socialist economies (ibid.:151), which do not quite convey the up-close/lo-

cal aspect with which he defined the notion at the outset. If community can be a *gesellschaft* as well as a *gemeinschaft*, then the market itself (e.g., the European Common Market[4]) is a community, and Gudeman's edifice
collapses.

Similarly diffuse is his definition of the "value domain"
that he calls *base*, which consists of "a community's *shared
interests*, which include lasting resources (such as land
and water), produced things, and ideational constructs
such as knowledge, technology, laws, practices, skills, and
customs" (ibid.:7). The base, he continues, comprises cultural beliefs and locally defined values that are embodied
in goods, services, and ideologies and that "express identity in community" (ibid.:8). The close connection between community and base is underlined by Gudeman's
observation that "maintaining the base and accumulating
capital epitomize the different projects of community and
market" (ibid.:10; cf. p. 33). After having offered *commons* as synonymous with base, he declares that "without
a commons, there is no community; without a community, there is no commons" (ibid.:27). The astonishing range
of examples includes scholarly knowledge, natural resources, a species of snail, a sacred mountain, talismans,
yoghurt culture, and the Crown Jewels (ibid.:28) – i.e.,
anything, it seems, that can serve as a common reference

---

[4] It is noteworthy that the European Union in several of its
constituent languages evokes the rhetoric of community and
gemeinschaft, reminding us that the ideological foundations of
"imagined communities" are far from trivial matters.

point for some kind of social category in some kind of context.

It is difficult to imagine something that could *not* qualify as base or commons in this sense. But then we are told that Gudeman's base or commons corresponds closely to Marcel Mauss's concept of *sacra* and to Annette Weiner's concept of "inalienable possessions" (ibid.:49, note 1), which is difficult to reconcile, for instance, with the above-mentioned assertion (ibid.:7) that it includes "produced things." The confusion continues when *sacra* are said to include "purchased marks of identity" such as cars, hairstyles, and clothing (ibid.:30). Rather than enumerating all these contradictory examples – and classifying cars with sacred mountains and hairstyles with Crown Jewels – would it not have been simpler (and more illuminating) to adopt, for example, Igor Kopytoff's (1986) observation that *processes* of sacralization and commoditization occur in a variety of cultural contexts? Yes, specific cars and items of clothing can become "sacred" to particular people, but let us not forget that they are generally prototypical commodities. The market for used cars suggests that automobiles are not exactly what Mauss or Weiner had in mind. It seems that Gudeman confuses, on one hand, people's propensity to adopt irreplaceable (and often individual) reference-points for identity – whether specific objects, places, or other people (cf. Hornborg 2001:208) – with a community's recognition of common resources, on the other.

A fundamental problem with Gudeman's definition of base is that it makes no effort to analytically distinguish between phenomena serving as moral symbols of identity and as sources of material sustenance (Gudeman 2001:29). Anthropologists are well aware that the latter can serve as the former – and increasingly, with tourism, also vice versa – but this does not warrant conflating them to the point of dissolving any analytical distinction between them. The concept of base or *foundation* that Gudeman retrieved from fieldwork in Panama and Colombia refers to "the material parts of a group's resources" (ibid.:38). His analysis of the Latin American notion of *fuerza* (ibid.:36–37)[5] as cognate to the physiocrats' emphasis on soil fertility – i.e., as a *material* parameter externalized by the neoclassical obsession with exchange value – would have been wonderfully germane to contemporary discussions in ecological economics, had he not chosen to dissolve it into a fuzzy and much more general category of things not amenable to monetary quantification. It is true that there are both material *and* moral dimensions of economy that the neoclassical model has made invisible, but let us look at these two kinds of substantive "externalities" separately, and show how they may be connected, before throwing them into the same bag. It is arguable that the neoclassical exclusion of material parameters (such as energy, soil quality, or labor time) from consideration goes hand in hand with the disregard of moral issues (such as whether exchange is unequal and to the systematic detriment of one party), and that the apotheosis of market evaluation in fact serves

[5] For an extended discussion, see Stephen Gudeman and Alberto Rivera, 1990:18–38.

ideologically to represent all exchange as equal. *These* are the kinds of issues that I would like to see economic anthropology address, but they require that an analytical distinction between the material and the symbolic is maintained rather than dissolved in amorphous categories such as Gudeman's notion of "base." Given the wide variety of phenomena that Gudeman uses to exemplify his concepts of community and base, I find it very difficult to see his distinction between base and capital (e.g., ibid.:121, 147). In which sense is capital *not* to be considered a base?

Another analytical move that I find confusing is the underlying conflation of the duality of community versus market with the distinction between the substantive and the formal. I can see how emphasis on community and "base" can be identified with a substantivist stance, and market with a formalist, but their simple conflation leads to a confusion of logical types. Community versus market is a distinction between different kinds of rationalities or actual behavior, whereas substantive versus formal is a distinction between different ways of conceptualizing or *narrating* behavior. Gudeman's polarities attempt to straddle the issue by suggesting that substantivists and formalists each have their own empirical territories. To the extent that Sahlins (1976) and Gudeman himself in *Economics as Culture* long ago exposed the underlying epistemological contradiction between substantivists and formalists in terms of the politics of abstraction, this fundamental ideological difference remains with us today and cannot be circumvented by trying to divide human behavior into two spheres to be studied with separate analytical tool kits. Formalists will undoubtedly continue to argue that their abstract and tautological models are applicable to virtually *all* human behavior, and substantivists that *no* human behavior is so disembedded as to make cultural contextualization superfluous. For instance, when Gudeman explains that "exchanges in community are different [from market exchange], for they revolve about ways of dividing a shared base, are guided by multiple values, and have to do with fashioning identities as well as material life" (Gudeman 2001:52), he seems oblivious of decades of studies, following Baudrillard and Bourdieu, showing how the consumption of market commodities is precisely about "fashioning identities." Striking a good bargain and fashioning identities need not be separate spheres of existence but different aspects of the same act. It is one thing to discuss the tension between community and market as sometimes antagonistic rationalities – and perhaps to observe that money and market logic may have saturated more and more of our lives in recent centuries (cf. ibid.:144) – and another thing to discuss competing models (substantive versus formal) for explaining a specific behavior. In the former case, we would need to investigate whether substantive, up-close/local/personal motives are actually being eclipsed or marginalized by far-distant/abstract/impersonal motives; in the latter, we would be dealing with the extent to which specific human motives can be meaningfully subsumed within highly abstract and formalized models. I am not suggesting that the two issues are unrelated,[6] only that we need to be able to address them separately.

Well into the second half of his book, Gudeman (ibid.:97) launches a promising critique of the conventional market model, with its focus on efficiency and rationality, for not being able to account for accumulation of monetary profit. Pure trade, he says, may be unbalanced "when assessed by a chosen metric," implying that "the gain of one actor must be another's loss," but *monetary* profit is something else and must be complemented with a theory of value. He then reviews various models that resort to theories of value to explain profit, from mercantilism through physiocracy to Ricardo and Marx. For mercantilists, physiocrats, and even the early Ricardo – as for several ethnographically reported groups, particularly in Latin America – *nature* is the ultimate source of value and profit a measure of the success of certain actors in appropriating their share of the limited good. In all these cases, the fundamental logic of the economy remains a zero-sum game. The decisive break with this cosmology was Ricardo's labor theory of value, published in *The Principles* in 1817, which made humans the agents of

[6] One obvious way in which they are related is through the medium of money itself, which represents a means of transforming or manifesting the formalist narrative into substantive behavior. In making virtually everything commensurable and interchangeable, general-purpose money transfers Economic Man from the imaginary to the real. In this sense, modernization has implied an implementation of the formalist model. This general perspective, of course, is new neither to Gudeman nor to conventional economists (ibid.:94).

value and profit. Marx later elaborated this perspective in his theory of capitalist exploitation of labor, according to which the capitalist pays for the exchange value of labor in order to control its use value in production. Marx's fundamental point was that labor can generate more market value than the cost of maintaining it (wages), and that capitalists can profit from the difference.[7] Gudeman shows, however, that even Marx ultimately ascribed this generative capacity of human labor to nature. Like the mercantilists, physiocrats, and early Ricardo, Marx saw value and profit as ultimately given by nature, "although once within circulation it could be transferred through modes of predation, such as financial or political power" (ibid.:101).

Neoclassical theory is different, Gudeman adds. There is no need for an exogenous nature in the "derivational" models of standard economics. But rather than ally himself with the ecological economists (and with the Colombian peasants with whom he has had long conversations on "the strength of the earth") to challenge the standard model, Gudeman assembles his own contribution to it, viz. that value and profit are created by *innovations* establishing what he calls a "productivity niche" (ibid.:105). From this (Schumpeterian?) perspective, he

---

[7] Rather than ascribe to labor such generative powers it would seem simpler to say merely that a capitalist is able to sell the products of labor at a higher price than wages, or – simpler still – that the price of labor is cheaper than the price of its products. A merit of such a formulation is that it need not attribute a uniquely generative capacity to labor, but is equally applicable to other inputs such as energy and raw materials.

chooses to dismiss Marx's occasional references to the ultimate origin of value as a gift of nature as a mystification (ibid.:106). A major problem with the now defunct socialist economies, he concludes, was that they did not foster innovation (ibid.:154). The identification of this "problem" sounds familiar and not very innovative, but to hear it from an anthropologist is perhaps the real novelty.

Gudeman's concluding questions for "today's debates on political economy" (ibid.:155) are more significant than the answers provided in this book. Basically, he argues, we should ask ourselves what we want to produce and distribute through the market and through community, respectively, and how these two "realms of value" should be mixed together. These do indeed seem to be the fundamental questions for a sustainable development, and they may require quite different answers than the ones provided by any of the economic systems of the twentieth century. Will politicians eventually need to confront the mantra of unfettered market forces by explicitly positing incommensurable values? Agricultural policies in Europe and North America indicate that *land* or *landscapes* are already implicitly treated as a collective base or *sacra* for industrial nation states, but when will we hear politicians or economists openly admitting it? And if they do admit it, what is to stop us from demanding that other fundamental values should be similarly immunized from the logic of market forces, such as food, health, education, housing, or social security (ibid.:161)? Will such basic resources for community survival require an economic sphere of their own, distinct from and insulated against global capital flows? How might the money system and other social institutions be redesigned to accomplish such a distinction? Should we be looking at ongoing experiments with alternative currencies, barter clubs, and informal economies as a means of forging a space for community in a world increasingly dominated by the market (ibid.:160)?

Gudeman briefly discusses the environment in these terms (ibid.:156), but it is obvious that he has not followed the past two decades of work in ecological economics. It is true that gross domestic output in industrial nations like the U.S. has been expanding much faster than their output measured in tons, leading many environmental economists to postulate a general trend toward *dematerialization*, but studies in material flow analysis instead suggest a systematic *displacement* of environmental loads from richer to poorer countries, much as advocated by Lawrence Summers more than a decade ago.[8] Gudeman heroically challenges the inclination of environmental economists to assign the environment a price – thus transforming "base to capital" – but makes no mention of the years of debate on *natural capital* and the antagonism between "strong" versus "weak" definitions of sustainability. Similarly ingenuous is his concern that economic globalization disconnects "profit centers from production and the nation that hosts a processing plant" (ibid.:157), presented as a loosening of "morality" and "commitment," indicating that Gudeman's idea of morality in economics

[8] The infamous "Lawrence Summers memo" can be downloaded from the Internet.

means keeping profits in industrial areas. There is no mention of the literature on unequal exchange in the world system suggesting that industrial "production" is a misnomer from the perspective of both ecology and global equity (e.g., Bunker 1985). This is certainly much more than an issue of intellectual property rights (cf. Gudeman 2001:157), as it raises fundamental questions about non-monetary metrics crucial to industrial accumulation but systematically ignored by standard economics.

Even the final page of *The Anthropology of Economy* exhibits this pervasive contrast between conventionality and diffuseness of analysis, on one hand, and politically highly relevant questions, on the other. Again, offering the 280-million strong nation of the United States as a "community" is at odds with the up-close/local definition Gudeman gave us at the outset. Yet, his final comments on the contested relation between market and non-market are pertinent indeed. The conversation on how to delineate community versus market, he says, "must take place outside the market discourse," for "we ought not let ourselves be persuaded that the coin has only one side" (ibid.:163). He then offers "the anthropology of economy" as a source of tools for such conversations. I could not agree more, but economic anthropology is not just a matter of presenting cross-cultural data – of which there are impressively many in this book – but of being able to frame these data in terms of categories that escape the confines of standard, Western economic thought. Gudeman does make a plea for moderating the neoliberal obsession with market forces, but that is about as far as he is able to distance himself from conventional economists, and it has in fact been done, for example, by a great number of institutionalists/substantivists and Marxists for a very long time. I would like, rather, to see an economic anthropology that seriously shakes the foundations of neoclassical (*and* Marxist) economic ideology by deconstructing its basic categories (such as "price," "profit," "value") in the light of cross-cultural comparison and perhaps also conversations with radically alternative economic paradigms such as are being advanced within ecological economics. In *The Anthropology of Economy*, Gudeman exploits very little of the potential for defamiliarizing cultural critique inherent in economic anthropology. This is a pity, because one possible next step that he could have taken beyond *Economics as Culture* and *Conversations in Colombia* would have been to trace the genealogy of neoclassical economic theory in terms of the political position of its founding fathers (such as the successful stockbroker David Ricardo) in the center of the colonial world system. The Ricardian shift from nature to labor as perceived sources of value certainly deserves to be interpreted in this perspective – i.e., economics not only as culture but also as *ideology* – since it has effectively excluded considerations of ecologically unequal exchange from our field of vision. Economic anthropology needs to ask itself why some of its leading proponents still to a very large extent adhere to a world view and terminology that was developed by stock brokers to explain their financial success in early nineteenth-century Britain, even as they attempt to comprehed the views and practices of the peripheral peoples whose natural resources and impoverishment were the basis of that success.

At the very end of his 1986 book *Economics as Culture*, Gudeman offered some *Reflections* which deserve to be quoted at some length:

> In all living societies humans must maintain themselves by securing energy from the environment. Although this life-sustaining process amounts only to a rearranging of nature, a transforming of materials from one state or appearance to another, humans make something of this activity. What they make of it has been the subject of this study. The creation of entropy may be constituted as productivity, a surplus, creativity, the ancestors, labor or even a sacrifice.
>
> ... Any set of economic constructions is a kind of mystification or ideology. ...
>
> The presence of other economic models also poses a threat, for knowledge of another construction leads to doubt about the ultimate validity of one's own. Universal models in economic anthropology represent a rejection of this doubt, for through a form of cultural reflexivity, they would assimilate others to us. ...
>
> But such self-projections are themselves of anthropological interest, for in his reflexive practices the universal modeler rejoins the world of all modelers. (Gudeman 1986, op. cit.:154–155)

In 1986, it seems, the only master narrative regarding economic activities that Gudeman was prepared to accept as non-ideological was the Second Law of Thermodynamics.[9] The universal modeler in economics could not

[9] The Second Law of Thermodynamics – sometimes referred to as the Entropy Law – states that any conversion of energy must imply a net reduction of order (i.e., increase in disorder, or entropy) in the universe. Nicholas Georgescu-Roegen (1971) showed that economic processes are not exempt from this law.

legitimately claim to have a privileged perspective vis-à-vis other, "local" modelers. Fifteen years later, in *The Anthropology of Economy*, Gudeman seems to have returned to the universalist project. He may be right in that a truly comparative economic anthropology does require abstractions, but my objections concern the nature of these abstractions. If we are going to have to use abstractions in the comparative study of human livelihood, as an anthropologist I would strongly advise against simply adopting Ricardo's (or even Schumpeter's) terminology. The cosmology of Gudeman's informants in Colombia, in fact, seems much better aligned with the Second Law of Thermodynamics than either Ricardo or Marx are. Their insights about economic processes could serve as a point of

The economic "production" of (cultural) order thus implies a destruction of (natural) order through the dissipation of concentrated matter and energy. This need not be a problem in itself, as long as we are dealing with pre-industrial economies based on solar energy and recycled materials, but should be a crucial consideration in our understanding of industrial societies based on the appropriation of finite stocks of energy and materials from their hinterlands. The accumulation of industrial infrastructure ("development") in world system centers relies on exchange with their peripheries that is unquestionably "unequal" in the sense that it implies net transfers of physical "order" or negentropy ("negative entropy"). I have argued that it is no coincidence that measurements approximating what Gudeman's Colombian informants call the "strength of the land" were abandoned in the economic theories that emerged in Ricardo's England. To this day, the perspective of neoclassical economic theory effectively rules out any questions regarding the extent to which the achievements of labor and capital in industrial economies are subsidized by the appropriation of natural resources ("land") from non-industrial sectors of the world economy (cf. Hornborg 2001).

departure for a truly critical economic anthropology, generating a completely different set of abstractions, geared not to *making* profits on the stock exchange but to *demystifying* them.

REFERENCES

Bunker, Stephen G. 1985. *Underdeveloping the Amazon: Extraction, Unequal Exchange, and the Failure of the Modern State.* Chicago: University of Chicago Press.

Marcus, George E., and Michael M. J. Fischer. 1986. *Anthropology as Cultural Critique: An Experimental Moment in the Human Sciences.* Chicago: University of Chicago Press.

Georgescu-Roegen, Nicholas. 1971. *The Entropy Law and the Economic Process.* Cambridge, Mass.: Harvard University Press.

Gudeman, Stephen. 1986. *Economics as Culture: Models and Metaphors of Livelihood.* London: Routledge & Kegan Paul.

—. 2001. *The Anthropology of Economy: Community, Market, and Culture.* Oxford: Blackwell.

Gudeman, Stephen, and Alberto Rivera. 1990. *Conversations in Colombia: The Domestic Economy in Life and Text.* Cambridge: Cambridge University Press.

Harvey, David. 1996. *Justice, Nature and the Geography of Difference.* Oxford: Blackwell.

Hornborg, Alf. 2001. *The Power of the Machine: Global Inequalities of Economy, Technology, and Environment.* Walnut Creek: AltaMira/Rowman & Littlefield.

Kopytoff, Igor. 1986. "The Cultural Biography of Things: Commoditization as Process," *The Social Life of Things: Commodities in Cultural Perspective,* ed. Arjun Appadurai, pp. 64–92. Cambridge: Cambridge University Press.

Sahlins, Marshall D. 1976. *Culture and Practical Reason.* Chicago: University of Chicago Press.

THE PITFALLS OF POSTMODERN ECONOMICS

REMARKS ON A PROVOCATIVE PROJECT

LARS PÅLSSON SYLL

Stephen Gudeman's thought-provoking and original book *The Anthropology of Economy* endeavors to establish economic anthropology as a discipline overarching political economy and economic philosophy. In this review essay I will offer some remarks from a perspective of methodology and science theory about this project and the basic conditions for its feasibility.

My critique of Gudeman will be directed mostly at what I perceive to be a questionable conflation of economy, culture, and community. I also question – from a scientific realist perspective – some postmodern/relativistic arguments underlying Gudeman's vision and argue for a realist science directed towards finding depth (structural) explanations. In the later sections of the essay I will scrutinize and criticize some of Gudeman's interpretations of parts of the history of economic thought. Here I will argue that he has misread some of the classics and therefore misrepresents important concepts such as "innovation" and "profit."

Although I will question some of the arguments in Gudeman's book, it must also be stressed how much valuable reasoning the work encompasses. Principally, it sheds light on the limited applicability of standard economic analysis. This is founded on unrealistic and reductionist premises and does not adequately take into account the fact that the economy is an open system and therefore cannot be treated with closed models that fundamentally exclude the consideration of cultural and institutional factors (cf. Pålsson Syll 2001; Lawson 1997).

Though there is a tendency in Gudeman's book to generalize its findings, as though the theoretical model applies to all societies at all times, I would still argue that the exemplifications the author uses really work as a healthy antidote to over-generalized and ahistorical neo-classical economics. Time has its own dimension, and its effect on an analysis must modify the whole theoretical system and not just be added as an unsystematic appendage. True dynamics is always historic, and acting like the baker's apprentice who, having forgotten to add yeast to the dough, throws it into the oven afterwards, is not enough.

By de-familiarizing traditional economic concepts, Gudeman also – in a way much akin to Kuhnian paradigmatic changes – makes us see beyond what we take for granted through the very structure of our languages, models, and theories. By using a kind of deductive detective work Gudeman helps us discover the hidden logic in what seems to be self-evident in modern society and shows us that there is no strictly economic rationality – only a totalizing, historical and social rationality.

This said, let me now start by commenting on the problem Gudeman is working on – to construct a theory of the functioning and evolution of economy.

SOCIAL SCIENCES AND EXPLANATION

One of the most important tasks of social sciences is to explain the events, processes, and structures that take place and act in society. But the researcher cannot stop at this. As a consequence of the relations and connections that the researcher finds, a will and demand arise for critical reflection on the findings. To show that unemployment depends on rigid social institutions or adaptations to European economic aspirations for integration, for instance, constitutes at the same time a critique of these conditions. It also entails an implicit critique of other explanations that one can show to be built on false beliefs. The researcher can never be satisfied with establishing that false beliefs exist but must go on to seek an explanation for why they exist. What is it that maintains and reproduces them? To show that something causes false beliefs – and to explain why – constitutes at the same time a critique of that thing.

This I think is something particular to the humanities and social sciences. There is no full equivalent in the natural sciences, since the objects of their study are not fundamentally created by human beings in the same sense as the objects of study in social sciences. We do not criticize apples for falling to earth in accordance with the law of gravitation.

The explanatory critique that constitutes all good social science thus has repercussions on the reflective person in society. Digesting the explanations and understandings that social sciences can provide means a simultaneous questioning and critique of one's self-understanding and the actions and attitudes it gives rise to. Science can play an important emancipating role in this way. Human beings can fulfill and develop themselves only if they do not base their thoughts and actions on false beliefs about reality. Fulfillment may also require changing fundamental structures of society. Understanding of the need for this change may issue from various sources like everyday praxis and reflection as well as from science.

Explanations of societal phenomena must be subject to criticism, and this criticism must be an essential part of the task of social science. Social science has to be an explanatory critique. The researcher's explanations have to constitute a critical attitude toward the very object of research, society. Hopefully, the critique may result in proposals for how the institutions and structures of society can be constructed. The social scientist has a responsibility to try to elucidate possible alternatives to existing institutions and structures.

In a time when scientific relativism is expanding, it is important to keep up the claim for not reducing science to a pure discursive level. We have to maintain the Enlightenment tradition of thinking of reality as principally independent of our views of it and of the main task of science as studying the structure of this reality. Perhaps the most important contribution a researcher can make is to reveal what this reality that is the object of science actually looks like.

Science is made possible by the fact that there are structures that are durable and are independent of our knowledge or beliefs about them. There exists a reality beyond our theories and concepts of it. It is this independent reality that our theories in some way deal with. Contrary to positivism, I cannot see that the main task of science is to detect event-regularities among observed facts. Rather, that task must be conceived as identifying the underlying structure and forces that produce the observed events.

The problem with positivist social science is not that it gives the wrong answers, but rather that in a strict sense it does not give answers at all. Its explanatory models presuppose that the social reality is "closed," and since social reality is fundamentally "open," models of that kind cannot explain anything of what happens in such a universe. Positivist social science has to postulate closed conditions to make its models operational and then – totally unrealistically – impute those closed conditions to society's real structure.

SOCIETY AND INDIVIDUAL

In the face of the kind of methodological individualism and rational choice theory that dominate positivist social science we have to admit that even if knowing the aspirations and intentions of individuals is a necessary prerequisite for giving explanations of social events, it is far from sufficient. Even the most elementary "rational" actions in society presuppose the existence of social forms that it is not possible to reduce to the intentions of individuals.

The overarching flaw with methodological individualism and rational choice theory is basically that they reduce social explanations to purportedly individual characteristics. But many of the characteristics and actions of the individual originate in and are made possible only through society and its relations. Society is not reducible to individuals, since the social characteristics, forces, and actions of the individual are determined by pre-existing social structures and positions. Even though society is not a volitional individual, and the individual is not an entity given outside of society, the individual (actor) and the society (structure) have to be kept analytically distinct. They are tied together through the individual's reproduction and transformation of already given social structures.

Here I think that Gudeman falters in *The Anthropology of Economy*. In orthodox economics, the economy is treated as a sphere that can be analyzed as if it were outside community, and in the well-known works of Polanyi – distinguishing between the formal and substantive meanings of economy – it was argued that the economy really had to be treated as something embedded in the community (see Polanyi 1944). When it was not, the disembedded economy had destructive repercussions. Building on Granovetter's critique of the "oversocialized" conception of human action, among others, Gudeman argues that economy *consists* of what he calls "community" and "market," and that economic relations are constituted within these realms and four "value domains" that he terms "base," "social relationships," "trade," and "accumulation" (cf. Granovetter 1985).

I will not go into the details of his model of economy but only note that I find it problematic to conflate economy, culture, and community in this way. It reminds me of the debate among sociologists on the age-old agent-structure problem, which some have tried to solve precisely by collapsing them into each other. A theory of economy (or society) that merely offers a resolution of different spheres in the homogeneity of "economy" is not very illuminating. It provides few if any indications of the pertinences of the distinctions that have to be made between the different levels at which these spheres (relations, structures, entities, etc.) exist. Collapsing them into one entity does not allow us to see clearly the forms of autonomy and interdependencies that prevail among the spheres. Total containment of culture and community within economy dissolves in a false way the tensions and dialectics that signify these different entities.

I think this conflation may also be problematic because it somehow takes away the basis for distinguishing between different sciences, that each possesses its own object of study. Although I am for transgressing often-artificial academic borders, I am doubtful whether this is the way to do it. Although economic anthropology may encompass much of what has formerly been done in economics, economic history, sociology, and cultural studies, I still think that these sciences are specific sciences operating at specific levels of abstraction and explaining particular differences that cannot be captured at the different level at which Gudeman's general and universal economic anthropological theory is situated. When studying societies and economies we have to be able to distinguish among different spheres, because it is the tension and dialectic between them that often is their prime mover. These spheres and the study of them have a relative autonomy, and to analyze them we have to take hold of their own levels.

Gudeman argues that "material action may be constructed through religious, social, or other 'non-economic' practices from which they cannot be separated" (op. cit.:4). This pinpoints the problem. Everything gets conflated into undifferentiated "practices," and a real possibility of emergence is denied, since we are not given a leveled model of how human beings both reproduce and transform the economy. I would have preferred it if Gudeman, rather than *conflating* (as I argue he does) different spheres, had tried to establish the *linkages* between them.

With a non-reductionist approach we avoid both determinism and voluntarism. For although the individual in society is formed and influenced by social structures that he does not construct himself, he can as an individual influence and change the given structures in another direction through his own actions. In society the individual is situated in roles or social positions that give limited freedom of action (through conventions, norms, material restrictions, etc.), but at the same time there is no principal necessity that we must blindly follow or accept these limitations. However, as long as social structures and positions are reproduced (rather than transformed), the actions of the individual will have a tendency to go in a certain direction.

What makes knowledge in social sciences possible is the fact that society consists of social structures and positions that influence the individuals of society, partly through their being the necessary prerequisite for the actions of individuals but also because they dispose individuals to act (within a given structure) in a certain way. These structures constitute the "deep structure" of society.

RELATIVIST TENDENCIES

We have to acknowledge the ontological fact that the world is mind-independent. This does not in any way reduce the epistemological fact that we can only know what the world is like from within our languages, theories, or discourses. But that the world is epistemologically mediated by theories does not mean that it is the product of them.

Gudeman obviously holds another view on this issue, writing that "I began to see economy as constructed through folk models and metaphors ... I proposed that there was no underlying, 'true' model of economy, but multiple, meaningful formulations within particular cultures" (op. cit.:4). To my eyes this is far too postmodern/social constructivist/relativist.

Our observations and theories are concept-*dependent* without therefore necessarily being concept-*determined*. There exists an independent reality beyond our theories and concepts of it. Although we cannot apprehend it without using our concepts and theories, these are not the same as reality itself. Reality and our concepts of it are not identical. Social science is made possible by existing structures and relations in society that are continually reproduced and transformed by different actors.

STRUCTURE AND INDIVIDUAL

Social science is relational. It studies and uncovers the social structures in which individuals participate and position themselves. It is these relations that have enough continuity, autonomy, and causal power to endure in society and be the real object of knowledge in social science. It is also only in their capacity as social relations and positions that individuals can be given power or resources (or the lack of them). To be a chieftain, a capital-owner, or a slave is not an individual property of an individual, but can come about only when individuals are integral parts of certain social structures and positions. Social relations and contexts cannot be reduced to individual phenomena – just as a check presupposes a banking system and tribe-members presuppose a tribe.

THE RELEVANCE OF SCIENTIFIC ASSUMPTIONS

Explanations and predictions of social phenomena require theory constructions. Just looking for correlations between events is not enough. One has to get under the surface and see the deeper underlying structures and mechanisms that essentially constitute the social system.

Contrary to the well-known symmetry hypothesis, (see Chalmers 1976, chap. 1), I would also maintain that explanation and prediction are not the same. To explain something is to uncover the generative mechanisms behind an event, while prediction only concerns actual events and does not have to say anything about the underlying causes of the events in question. The barometer may be used for predicting today's weather changes. But these predictions are not explanatory, since they say nothing about the underlying causes.

Methodologically, this implies that the basic question one has to pose when studying social relations and events is what are the fundamental relations without which they would cease to exist. The answer will point to causal mechanisms and tendencies that act in the concrete contexts we study. Whether these mechanisms are activated and what effects they will have in that case is not possible to predict, since this depends on accidental and variable relations. Every social phenomenon is determined by a host of both necessary and contingent relations, and it is impossible in practice to have complete knowledge of these constantly changing relations. That is also why we can never confidently predict them. What we can do, through learning about the mechanisms of the structures of society, is to identify the driving forces behind them, thereby making it possible to indicate the direction in which things tend to develop.

SCIENTIFIC EXPLANATIONS

If we want the knowledge we produce to have practical relevance, the knowledge we aspire to and our methods have to adapt to our object of study. In social sciences – such as economics, history, or anthropology – we will never reach *complete* explanations. Instead we have to aim for *satisfactory* and *adequate* explanations.

As is well known, there is no unequivocal criterion for what should be considered a *satisfactory* explanation. All explanations (with the possible exception of those in mathematics and logic) are fragmentary and incomplete; self-evident relations and conditions are often left out so that one can concentrate on the nodal points. Explanations must, however, be real in the sense that they "correspond" to reality and are capable of being used.

The *relevance* of an explanation can be judged only by reference to a given *aspect* of a problem. An explanation is then relevant if, for example, it can point out the generative mechanisms that rule a phenomenon or if it can illuminate the aspect one is concerned with. To be relevant from the explanatory viewpoint, the adduced theory has to provide a good basis for believing that the phenomenon to be explained really does or did take place. One has to be able to say: "That's right! That explains it. Now I understand why it happened."

While positivism tries to develop a general *a priori* criterion for evaluation of scientific explanations, it would be better to realize that all we can try for is *adequate* explanations, which it is not possible to disconnect from the specific, contingent circumstances that are always incident to what is to be explained.

Here I think Gudeman goes wrong in that he clearly thinks his general model/theory is applicable to all kinds of societies and economies. The fact that most economies show a dialectical relationship between "market" and "community" does not take us any further than the neoclassical economists' insistence that all known economies have had to deal with scarcity in some form or other. I think we have to be more modest and acknowledge that our models and theories are time-space relative.

Besides being an aspect of the situation in which the event takes place, an explanatory factor ought also to be causally *effective*; that is, one has to consider whether the event would have taken place even if the factor had not existed. And it also has to be causally *deep*. If event *e* would have happened without factor *f*, then this factor is not deep enough. Triggering factors, for instance, often do not have this depth. And by contrasting different factors with each other we may find that some are irrelevant (without causal depth).

Without the requirement of depth, explanations most often do not have practical significance. This requirement leads us to the nodal point against which we have to take measures to obtain changes. If we search for and find fundamental structural causes for unemployment, we can hopefully also take effective measures to remedy it.

WHY EXPLANATIONS ARE IMPORTANT

Scientific theories (ought to) do more than just describe event-regularities. They also analyze and describe the mechanisms, structures, and processes that exist. They try to establish what relations exist between these different phenomena and the systematic forces that operate within the different realms of reality.

Explanations are important within science, since the choice between different theories hinges in large part on their explanatory powers. The most reasonable explanation for one theory's having greater explanatory power than others is that the mechanisms, causal forces, structures, and processes it speaks of, really do exist.

LEVELS OF EXPLANATION

When studying the relation between different factors, a social scientist is usually prepared to admit the existence of a reciprocal interdependence between them. One is seldom prepared, on the other hand, to investigate whether this interdependence might follow from the existence of an underlying causal structure. This is really strange. The actual configurations of a river, for instance, depend of course on many factors. But one cannot escape the fact that it flows downhill and that this fundamental fact influences and regulates the other causal factors. Not to come to grips with the underlying causal power that the direction of the current constitutes can only be misleading and confusing.

All explanations of a phenomenon have preconditions that limit the number of alternative explanations. These preconditions significantly influence the ability of the different potential explanations to really explain anything. If we have a system where underlying structural factors control the functional relations between the parts of the system, a satisfactory explanation can never disregard this precondition. Explanations that take the parts (micro-explanations) as their point of departure may well *describe* how and through which mechanisms something takes place, but without the structure we cannot *explain* why it happens.

But could one not just say that different explanations

94

– such as individual and structural – are different, without a need to grade them as better or worse? I think not. That would be too relativistic. For although we are dealing with two different kinds of explanations that answer totally different questions, I would say that the structural most often answers the more relevant questions. In social sciences we often search for explanations of events because we want to be able to avoid or change certain outcomes. Giving individualistic explanations does not make this possible, since they only state sufficient but not necessary conditions. Without knowing the latter we cannot prevent or avoid these undesirable social phenomena.

All kinds of explanations in empirical sciences are pragmatic. We cannot just say that one type is *false* and another is *true*. Explanations have a function to fulfill, and some are *better* and others *worse* at this. Even if individual explanations can show the existence of a pattern, the pattern as such does not constitute an explanation. We want to be able to explain the pattern per se, and for that we usually require a structural explanation. By studying statistics of the labor market, for example, we may establish the fact that everyone who is at the disposal of the labor market does not have a job. We might even notice a pattern, that people in rural areas, old people, and women are often jobless. But we cannot explain with these data why this is a fact and that it may even be that a certain amount of unemployment is a functional requisite for the market economy. The individualistic frame of explanation gives a false picture of what kind of causal relations are at hand, and *a fortiori* a false picture of what needs to be done to make a change possible. For that, a structural explanation of the kind mentioned above is required.

TRADE AND PROFIT

Gudeman describes how markets are always embedded in a cultural and social context, and he is therefore critical of the neoclassical market model. But not so much on account of its detachment from reality as for its failure to account for accumulation and profits.

As all students of economics know, the *origin* of surplus and profits is a contested area. Gudeman relates the source of profits to capital accumulation and contends that it has to do with the process of "value creation" and should not be perceived as a "profit upon alienation" (which was the theory given, for example, by the Mercanitilists, Cantillon and James Stewart) or as a "gift of nature" (cf. Pålsson Syll 2002, chap. 4; Meek 1973; Dobb 1973).

So far so good. The problematic point arises when Gudeman says that the physiocrats and Marx adhered to the latter theory and regarded surplus values and profits as a "gift of nature."

Starting with Quesnay *et consortes*, it is nowadays well-known that their surplus – "*le produit net*" – is *not* conceived of as a gift of nature. Wealth for the physiocrats has both a material ("natural") and a value side. Unfortunately, scholars often overlook this by one-sidedly over-emphasizing the importance of *Tableau économique*. In this Quesnay uses a more distinctly material concept, but the different versions of the tableau do *not* give a fair picture of the whole theory that had been worked out. It is especially important to note that when Quesnay constructed his different *Tableaux économiques* he presupposed that those changes which the physiocrats advocated had already been implemented – the use of the best possible technique, "*la grande culture*" (a heavily capitalized agriculture with England standing as a model), free trade, and so on.

Profit in the physiocratic theory is proportional to the expenses, and is not any kind of higher wage, but an entrepreneurial remuneration. After paying his costs of production, taxes ("*la taille*"), and rent ("*le bail*") – which together make up the fundamental price ("*le prix fondamental*") – the cultivator keeps his profit after selling his products at market price ("*le prix du vendeur*"). The profit of the cultivator is dependent on both these prices, and since the technical costs of production, taxes, and rent are taken as given, the profit is really a residual that depends only on the market price.

The physiocratic concept of profits therefore comes very close in fact to being a theory of profit-alienation – buying cheap and selling expensive. What saves their concept from ending up in that cul-de-sac is mainly that the physiocrats also perceive the possibility of the market price being influenced by technical changes in production taking place to reduce the fundamental price.

If the market price is high enough to give a profit and incite new investments, the physiocrats call it "*le prix bon*." So even if the physiocrats' profit is equivalent to a profit-alienation, it is not a given percent of the invested capital.

Profit – which only accrues to the agricultural farmer

– plays a unique role in physiocracy. It is the source of accumulation and a decisive factor in the growth process. Although it is an exclusively agricultural phenomenon in the physiocrats' theory, it is *not* – more than perhaps in a metaphorical sense – a "gift of nature." It fundamentally depends on social relations and the urge of the peasants to invest in capital-intensive production. And on the fact that in agriculture, "demand is always higher than supply" (Quesnay, in Oncken 1888:551).[1]

Even more perplexing is Gudeman's allegation when it comes to Marx. According to Marx, the origin of profit is in the difference between labour and labour power. To Marx, labour power is a specific commodity, since in "contradistinction to the case of other commodities, there enters into the determination of the value of labour-power a historical and moral element" (Marx 1954:68). And it "may be expanded, or contracted, or altogether extinguished, so that nothing remains but the physical limit … We can only say that, the limits of the working day being given, the *maximum* of profit corresponds to the *physical minimum of wages*; and that wages being given, the *maximum of profit* corresponds to such prolongation of the working day as is compatible with the physical forces of the labourer" (Marx 1947:50). With wages as with the length of the working day, "the nature of the exchange of commodities itself imposes no limits … Between equal rights force decides. Here is it that … the determination of what is a working-day presents itself as

---

[1] On physiocracy in general, see Pålsson Syll 2002, op. cit., chap. 4; Vaggi 1987; Vidonne 1986.

the result of a struggle between collective capital … and collective labour" (op. cit.:223–225). Marx never denies that capital and land are involved in creating commodities and *wealth*. But that does not imply that capital and land create *value*. That is only for labor to do. Value is created in the process of labor, where the value-creating potential of labor power is realized. Labor is the substance of value, but has itself no value. Value is an expression of *social* relations between men. To think it is an attribute of nature was according to Marx an expression of commodity fetishism.

Capitalism is founded on the social relation that capital and labor constitute. When the capital-owner buys labor power from the worker, he buys a commodity that becomes a capital in the process of production. The fact that the worker's individual consumption is subsumed in the circuit of capital does not change the fact that labor power is *not* a capital-product. It only means that it is a product of the worker's own consumption. In the process of production it is only use value that figures, and the variable capital as capital figures only in the exchange process preceding production.

It is *not* in its quality as value that labor power creates value, but only in its quality as use value, "the transcending movement."

So when Gudeman says that Marx sought a foundation for profits "outside the market domain" and that the capacity to produce profit was "nature's donation" (op. cit.:101), he is indeed off the mark. The source is *outside* the economy only in the sense that the reproduction of labor power is not a part of capital's circuit. But that in no way implies that to Marx profit was "exogenously given," as the several chapters of *Capital* describing and analyzing the extraction of relative surplus value clearly show.

In a way, Gudeman's attempt to reinterpret the physiocracy and Marx reminds me of Piero Sraffa's well-known attempt to reinterpret classical economic theory (see Kurz 2000; Pålsson Syll 2002, op. cit., chap. 12). But, like Sraffa, Gudeman fails to convince. The textual basis is not there. One or two disconnected quotations do not make up a convincing theoretical argument.

ON PROFITS AND UNCERTAINTY

Gudeman also presents his own theory of profit. Since it has a strong Schumpeterian flavor I will first try to set down the essentials of this view, before I move on to a critical discussion of Gudeman.

Against the classics' view of an abstract and undifferentiated capital stands Schumpeter's concept of the entrepreneur, which underlines the importance of conceptualizing the firm as actively striving to break with "the circular flow" and via innovations and new investments differentiate itself from the others. This concept may be used as a steppingstone for criticizing the use of equilibrium concepts in the analysis of economic development and evolution (see Schumpeter 1983 [1934]; Pålsson Syll 2002, op. cit., chap. 12).

According to Schumpeter, the entrepreneur is in possession of specific knowledge and skills. These are the firm's specific units of production. In contradistinction to the view of the classics, the firm is not satisfied with the normal, general rate of profit but strives actively to continually break new paths and develop "new methods and combinations," in pursuit of the quasi-rents that the classical analysis disregards by concentrating on static equilibrium in the long run. The competition between the firms is based upon the allocation and availability of the specific units of production, and new methods and techniques are spread only insofar as one can avail oneself of them.

Investments can therefore never have the classics' character of "hothouse." They are not simple reflexes of capital, but eminently firm-specific. This is also the reason why competition does not lead only to fast-growing firms having to content themselves with "normal" profits; in the long run – between the imaginary long-run equilibriums – one can acquire large "profit differentials."

Neoclassical theory assumes that firms in equilibrium may avail themselves of the usual interest on capital and nothing more. "Pure" profits are assumed to be zero, since genuine uncertainty (in the Knight-Keynes-Myrdal-Schumpeter-Shackle sense, not to be confused with probabilistically calculable "risk") is absent.[2] In a sequence of temporary equilibriums with "perfect foresight" we of course get the usual Walrasian inter-temporal equilibrium solution with zero profits (see Arrow and Hahn 1971, esp. chap. 3).

The greatness of Schumpeter is his questioning the unreal assumption upon which this profit-theory is built,

[2] On the difference between risk and uncertainty, see Knight 1921.

since, as he puts it, "the assumption that conduct is prompt and rational is in all cases a fiction" (op. cit., 1983 [1934]:80). In real life, profits are never equal to zero, since especially the assumptions of structural invariance and fulfilled expectations are unrealistic. The innovations of the entrepreneur transform the structure and break with the adaptive behavior through successful projects that give the initiator a "pure" profit through prices that are higher than the average costs of production that determine the market price. The "pure" profit is only temporary, since imitation and decreasing market-advantage are continually diminishing it. How long the "pure" profit exists depends fundamentally on how all-encompassing the diffusion- and entry-barriers are.

In the Schumpeterian vision it is the anticipated possibility of making profit that constitutes the incentive for the innovations and investments of the entrepreneur. It is via this that capitalism obtains its dynamic character, something that will never surface in the static general equilibrium models of the neoclassic or the long-run equilibrium models of the classics. This is also what makes Schumpeter's approach interesting to develop as a substitute for all-too-unrealistic economic models.

When Gudeman says that "Schumpeter's signal contribution was to connect the act of innovation to uncertainty" (op. cit.:104), this has to be qualified. Because, as I perceive it, a failure of Schumpeter's theory is that it maintains that the origin of the "pure" profit lies in the structural transformation *per se*, while I would say – with Knight – that this is so only when the transformation is *unpredicted*.

Now the main problem I have with Gudeman's "extended" Schumpeterian theory is that he plainly overstates its generality. First he states that profit – *tout court* – is created by innovations or "new combinations."[3] And then he states: "Normal profit is the return secured for innovations made in conditions of uncertainty." This is an unfortunate confusion, since what Gudeman calls (normal) profits is what economists – Schumpeter, Marx, and neoclassic – usually call "extra-profits," "supernormal profits," or "pure profits." Gudeman's inaccuracy might seem harmless, but it is not. The rationale behind the absent clear-cut distinction between profits and "pure" profits is that his theory is based on the assumption that continual innovation is the basis for *all* profits and economic growth.

Where does it go wrong? Perhaps here: Gudeman notes that in neoclassical economics profits do not exist in equilibrium (other than as interest and rent). Schumpeter shows – more realistically – that profit as a result of innovation exists in reality. I would say – as a non-neoclassical economist, anyway – that what he shows is that the hunt for extra-profits drives capitalism forward, but that profits in the real world could exist even if innovations were non-existent. Increased production, changes in distribution and demand-conditions can, of course, in themselves give rise to profits.

Gudeman acknowledges other ways of securing profits, of course, especially through three different forms of what he calls arbitrage. But although market power de-

---

[3] Op. cit., p. 102. See also page 120 where he states that "value and profit are created by innovation."

termines how long the entrepreneur will earn the super-normal "pure" profits, their social role is not really clear-cut. Keynes, for one, emphasized that uncertainty also gives birth to opportunities for speculation and therefore does not have to correspond to social productivity. This therefore should also be added to Gudeman's list of "arbitrage profits."

THE IMPORTANCE OF INNOVATIONS

In chapter seven, entitled "Profit on the Small," Gudeman further explores the meaning of innovation.

In *Business Cycles* (1939) Schumpeter simply defined innovation as "the setting up of a new production function" that covered "the case of a new commodity, as well as those of a new form of organization such as a merger, of the opening up of new markets, and so on." Innovation in the Schumpeterian sense consists of making "new combinations" that give rise to lower costs of production for the often newly established firms that use them. Economic development and transformation is an "evolutionary process" that is driven by the innovations and investments that the entrepreneurs make in anticipation of higher profits. This process of "creative destruction" revolutionizes the economic structure from within, "incessantly destroying the old one, incessantly creating a new one" (1976 [1943]:83). In Schumpeter's vision this innovation-driven development is "spontaneous and discontinuous change ... which forever alters and displaces the equilibrium state previously existing" (1983: 64).

Gudeman elaborates on Schumpeter's concept and especially emphasizes the fact that innovations do not take place in a vacuum, but on the contrary, have to "emerge within a heritage that they revise" (op. cit.: 111), since the innovator is embedded in a communal context. To Gudeman, innovations consist mainly of learning by doing, trial and error, "adjusting and accommodating," and he gives a very vivid and illustrative example of a potter in Guatemala.

I find this enlightening and an improvement on Schumpeter's rather "economistic" approach to innovation. But I would still like to suggest a complement, stressing unintentional innovations and their cumulative effects as well.

When people try to make use of the best methods of production available, one could imagine them, by pure stochastic chance and unintentionally, happening to do something a little bit different than foreseen. Finding that this perhaps makes the production cheaper – and given the mechanisms of "trial and error," "learning by doing," "practice makes perfect," and the socio-cultural preconditions of perceptive abilities, memory, cultural and social stability – we may even get an intergenerational transfer of innovations and *a fortiori* new technologies. Which shows that even piecemeal and unintentional change may give rise to cumulative innovational and technological effects.

So what I am saying is that innovation could *also* be perceived as essentially being a by-product, rather than only an intentional volitional act performed in anticipation of making profits. This "model" underlines the difficulty of uniting the prevalence of unpredictable and unintentional innovations with the neoclassical economist's faith in instrumental rationality.

Perhaps this is also what Gudeman is maintaining when he argues, "[T]he idea that instrumental calculations, using a single measuring rod, anchor the market is threatened by the innovation view of profit because of the lack of predictable outcome it suggests in the central activity of the market" (op. cit.:119). But it is not only the *outcome* of innovation that is unpredictable. The innovation *per se*, as I have argued, might to a large extent be conceived of as unintentional and unpredictable.

GLOBALIZATION AND THE ALTERNATIVES

In chapter eight Gudeman expands on previously presented ideas on values in production, trade, and use. People trade to maintain or expand what Gudeman calls "the base." But they may also make appropriations, and Gudeman gives interesting descriptions of how this process may lead to a community losing control over its base – leading to debasement – and its members having to enter the market. Countries in the "underdeveloped" world are basically dual-sector economies, and when they are integrated with the world market, this regularly leads both to unjust terms of trade and to unequal exchange of labor and natural resources.

I find this reasoning especially interesting, since I consider this the very basis for contemporary globalization, a new form of what Marx described as "original accumulation" in his *Capital*.

Gudeman also discusses different counter-strategies for communities and their members to sustain themselves and resist the dictates of the global market. Examples of this are exchange circuits (LETS), barter clubs, alternative currencies, and local communities. Together with the new information system, these make it possible to form new communities and, perhaps, new identities. But Gudeman is skeptical – especially when discussing the microcredit-system Grameen Bank – since he doubts that we can "foster community development as a precursor to economic growth" or that community is something that "can be planned" (op. cit.:139–140).

Gudeman is right, of course, that community is essentially a by-product. Planning community is a self-defeating strategy. This is not what is at issue here, however.

The increasing "informalization" of the economy – social economy, local economy, illegal work, and so on – is a symptomatic sign of the fact that people do not passively just await their destiny. The more the global economy expands, the more people, firms, and regions are also systematically excluded. But those who do not just want to live to consume, try in different ways to find ways to consume to live. Those who through their "place-confinement" are excluded from the global economy's all-encompassing inclusion – the poor, the marginalized, outcompeted, unprofitable – are looking out for new development trajectories. The goal is to win back their lives and take the future into their own hands by using a conscious "policy of the place." The "social economy" and new forms of democracy from below can increasingly make up the skeleton of a civil society that protects itself against the global economy's trespasses and pressures on the space of democracy. As one develops more power of one's own, one tries to build protective walls against the tide of global capital and a selective global division of labor.

Those who were formerly excluded now self-consciously choose exclusion as a strategy of survival. They are no longer satisfied with standing on tiptoe for the Market and silently watching the flexible global capital – without any other concern than capitalization of the universal equivalent in the form of money – walk away from the party and leave the garbage behind in the form of refuse, wrecked environment, and unemployment to be taken care of by the locals in both center and periphery.

People are beginning to understand that it is not self-evident that economic values should out-trump all other values. No one denies the inherent dynamics and strength of globalization. What market-fundamentalists often forget is that it also has a reverse side. To many people and countries, globalization is nothing but the apotheosis of inequality. To them it is self-evident that global financial markets and light-footed papers of value demanding instant dividends can no longer be allowed to dismantle democracy and welfare. Markets must be embedded in culture and institutions; otherwise they undermine their own existence by displacing the social stability they are founded on. If the global markets cannot be re-embedded, building local economies might be the only feasible way of immunization or disconnection from global markets.

CONCLUSION

Although in this review essay I have criticized the author of *The Anthropology of Economy* for some of his interpretations of important lineages in the history of economic thought, I would nevertheless want to stress that these doctrinal inadvertencies do not constitute a serious blow to his theoretical "vision" or detract from the book's value as a contribution to understanding economics and society. Those points just underline the importance of academic *akribeia* and of getting the antecedents right. When it comes to my more science-theoretical criticism of some postmodern and relativist strains in Gudeman's theoretical endeavor to construct a "universal" or "general" economic anthropology of the functioning and evolution of the economy – ranging from primitive and traditional societies to market societies in a globalized world – the cut is of course deeper. I am firmly convinced that *The Anthropology of Economy* would have been (even) more convincing – and not risked falling into the postmodern abyss of relativism – if it had been based on a more realist foundation.

REFERENCES

Arrow, Kenneth J., and Frank H. Hahn. 1971. *General Competitive Analysis*. San Francisco: Holden-Day.

Chalmers, Allan F. 1976. *What Is This Thing Called Science?* St. Lucia, Queensland: University of Queensland Press.

Dobb, Maurice. 1973. *Theories of Value and Distribution since Adam Smith*. Cambridge: Cambridge University Press.

Granovetter, Mark. 1985. "Economic Action and Social Structure: The Problem of Embeddedness," *American Journal of Sociology*, vol. 91, pp. 481–510.

Knight, Frank H. 1921. *Risk, Uncertainty and Profit*. London: London School of Economics.

Kurz, Heinz D. (ed.). 2000. *Critical Essays on Piero Sraffa's Legacy in Economics*. Cambridge: Cambridge University Press.

Gudeman, Stephen. 2001. *The Anthropology of Economy: Community, Market, and Culture*. Oxford: Blackwell.

Lawson, Tony. 1997. *Economics and Reality*. London: Routledge.

Marx, Karl. 1947. *Wages, Price and Profit*. Moscow: Progress Publishers.

—. 1954. *Capital*, vol. I. London: Lawrence & Wishart.

Meek, Ronald L. 1973. *The Precursors of Adam Smith*. London: J M Dent.

Oncken, August. 1888. *Ouevres Économiques et Philosophiques de Francois Quesnay*. Frankfurt.

Polanyi, Karl. 1944. *The Great Transformation*. New York: Holt, Rinehart.

Pålsson Syll, Lars. 2001. *Ekonomisk teori och metod [Economic Theory and Method]*. Lund: Studentlitteratur.

—. 2002. (third ed.) *De ekonomiska teoriernas historia [The History of Economic Theories]*. Lund: Studentlitteratur.

Schumpeter, Joseph A. 1983 [1934]. *The Theory of Economic Development*. New Brunswick: Transaction Publishers.

—. 1964 [1939]. *Business Cycles*. New York: McGraw-Hill.

—. 1976 [1943]. *Capitalism, Socialism and Democracy*. London: George Allen & Unwin.

Vaggi, Gianni. 1987. *The Economics of Francois Quesnay*. Basingstoke: Macmillan.

Vidonne, Paul. 1986. *La formation de la pensée économique*. Paris: Economica.

REALISM, RELATIVISM AND REASON

WHAT'S ECONOMIC ANTHROPOLOGY ALL ABOUT?

STEPHEN GUDEMAN

According to my critics, in *The Anthropology of Economy* I have committed opposed errors. Lars Pålsson Syll claims I have fallen into the pit of radical relativism and postmodernism. Salvation lies in adopting a "realist" epistemology. Alf Hornborg, however, accuses me of abandoning relativism for a modernist approach. He maintains I have been sucked into the endless hole of employing abstractions and spinning master narratives. Both are cross with me but for opposite reasons (even if they use a similar metaphor to dramatize my fallen state). I am tempted to suggest that they first settle their differences in a Roman arena, but Gert Helgesson's sympathetic reading prompts me to think my critics are irritated because they share the same view, which is threatened by mine. So, we need to "dig" into their accounts to find the source of their displeasure.[1]

[1] I am most appreciative to my colleague, Mischa Penn, for his many comments and suggestions on this essay.

We part ways principally over three issues: epistemology, local models, and the project of economic anthropology. For me, economic anthropology is fascinating because it forces us to reexamine our language, values, and everyday categories, especially in market societies where the economic spirit is prominent in practices and narratives about life. Leaving aside the details of their critiques – and I shall attend to them – my stern reviewers do not fully embrace a comparative and critical project precisely because they cling to a questionable epistemology. Pålsson Syll is aware of his affliction and embraces it. Hornborg displays its symptoms but denies the infection. (Helgesson is not afflicted but asks for more "reason" in my approach.) Every disease needs a name, so let's identify the Pålsson Syll–Hornborg malady as the search for certainty; its most resilient form is essentialism or foundationalism. In the case of my critics the symptoms are several. Both have adopted an older "science" view of the "natural" world: it consists of separate levels, to be analyzed by an appropriate discipline, with the layers composing a hierarchy of knowledge. Pålsson Syll and Hornborg apply this blueprint to society. Social life consists of separate self-organizing levels, such as the "individual" and "institutions," or the "symbolic" and the "material." These levels may be independent, as Hornborg proclaims, or "causally" linked in a hierarchy, as Pålsson Syll avers. Both Pålsson Syll and Hornborg are driven to banish ontological angst by positing an independent bottom level in society (without pits and holes) from which they can interpret and explain the remaining "facts" or "variables" of social life. There are other variations of the layer-cake view, however. Parsons famously divided the social world into four functions (or cells) and institutional orders, such as behavioral organism, personality, society, and culture.[2] Each cell contained four more divisions, and then more in a descending and more specialized order. Parsons claimed the different functional sectors of society were related through input/output connections. A more contemporary version presents society and economy as consisting of discrete layers with feedback among them (Ruttan 2003).

In contrast to the layer-cake view of my critics, I do not presume that society or economy is organized in levels, each of which is self-contained or self-organizing (essentialism) or all of which are tied to a final level (foundationalism). In place of assuming that we live in a coherent and systematic economy that is causally, functionally, or deductively organized, I hold that we find contingent and mixed constructions. Even if Pålsson Syll and Hornborg seem to hold opposed views because they utilize different foundations for analyzing economy, I think both are cross with me because I have been attacking the idea of essentialism or foundationalism.

Through economic anthropology I have been offering the perspective of local models. I contrast these to a universal model, which characterizes Pålsson Syll's and Hornborg's approach (Gudeman and Penn 1982; Gudeman 1986). The universal model, with its mechanisms

[2] The four functions were adaptation, goal-attainment, integration, and pattern-maintenance. The functions were principally carried out through different institutions: economy, polity, social order, and religion.

and levels, is coherent, consistent, and replicable. It has a bounded structure with rules of formation that range from derivations, to causal links, to deduction. Euclidean geometry, with axioms and derivations, offers one example of the clean consistency that makes universal models persuasive. Local models are worlds apart. They have no inherent structure and combine many rhetorical forms, such as analogy, metaphor, and abstraction, as well as means-to-ends calculation. Local models are a composite, always in the making, and malleable. Without limits, in the sense of being bounded by rules of inclusion, local models are a creative (and innovative) mix of images and ways of doing. Consisting of practices and narratives, they may be written, oral, or sketched in the earth. Ethnographically, I have found them presented in spoken discourse but also in myths and rituals.

Local models are situated, and several may be developed in a context; usually one is dominant, although even a salient local model may have variations. For example, Marx offered a finely honed model of capitalism that circles around the expenditure of labor: some might argue that it is contextually positioned from the perspective of an industrial laborer. Physiocracy was a school of modelers, with somewhat divergent visions, who focused on the land; their model was partially positioned from the standpoint of landowners in pre-Revolutionary France. (I shall return to these models, as both Pålsson Syll and Hornborg object to, and are disturbed by, the way I analyze them rhetorically.) Similarly, I once drew on a "dependency" model of economy to help illuminate ethnography from Panama, partly because that model was originally forged in the context of Latin American conditions; it employs a mix of images, such as "poles" and "peripheries." After that work was completed, a colleague and I presented our ethnography from the highlands of Colombia through the people's "house" model of the economy (Gudeman and Rivera 1990). These farmers use the image or metaphor of the house for their economic practices. Certainly, the anthropologist is also positioned with respect to local models; for example, one of my purposes in writing *The Anthropology of Economy* was to bring local models into a larger conversation or dialogue to enhance communication and critical reflection.

Most local models contain their own justification or claim to legitimacy. Pålsson Syll waves the red flag of "realism" as if it were the trump card in the limited deck from which he deals; he claims that realism justifies his structural view of economy. Hornborg hangs on to the laws of thermodynamics to legitimate his relativism. Part of my endeavor as an economic anthropologist is not only to illuminate local models, using whatever tools I can find, but to explore their legitimating stories that range from invoking the gods, God, the ancestors, and nature, to "correspondence" theories and "science."

In my view, universal models are one form of local model; however, they claim to be all-embracing. Because of their foundationalism, universal models also seem to have general applicability, but they are contextual. In *The Anthropology of Economy*, I criticize most market models for providing a partial picture of the total economy from which they have been abstracted. They also are levels models that would explain phenomena such as institutions (and sometimes all behavior) through derivations, deductions, or causal relations. Neither of my critics recognized the way this view of models informed *The Anthropology of Economy*, for the book revolves about their shifting mixes. In this respect, the anthropological encounter does not always take place between "us" and "others" but is within local situations, because we use several models even as we silence the contradictions. Thus, given this anthropological project of exploring local models, I shall turn first to a more detailed look at the epistemological problems in Pålsson Syll's and Hornborg's commentaries before listening to what Helgesson has to say and then addressing the derivative criticisms of my two critics.

THE WORLD ACCORDING TO PÅLSSON SYLL

Pålsson Syll asserts that a realist epistemology provides the only way to explain economic life. Like me, the reader may be puzzled that Pålsson Syll separates his commentary into two parts: a description of scientific realism in the first and a "correct" reading of economics texts in the second. But the sections are connected, because Pålsson Syll invokes his epistemological view in the first part to justify his critique of my observations about the language of Marx and the Physiocrats in the second. I welcome his comments because they mirror the uncomfortable relationship between contemporary anthropology and modern economics. So, I want to begin with a brief sketch of these disciplinary differences before addressing Pålsson Syll's realist epistemology.

Traditionally, anthropologists and economists had few

border fights because we studied "different" people (or so we thought): anthropologists were experts on the "primitive," small-scale, simpler societies; economists knew about market societies. The situation was never that simple; however, we lived with the fiction, kept to our own, and didn't talk to each other. But when anthropologists began to erase the division between "us" and "the others" and to examine the effects of market expansion and capitalism on "them," we encountered import barriers preventing entry of our goods. At much the same moment, economists were extending their analytical apparatus into domains that once "belonged" to us (Becker's work on the family is a well-known example). These breaches and invasions, as well as developments in studies of science, have brought our differences to the fore. Some (but not all) economists construct models that leave little room for local meanings and social reactions; and some offer predictions and prescriptions about economic behavior. Let us call this the top-down approach. In contrast, many (but not all) anthropologists offer descriptions of practices and people's representations to build a contextual view. We'll call this a bottom-up approach. If one side has tended to be axiomatic and prescriptive, the other has been more pragmatic and contextual, and lacking in predictions. For example, if a people say they must "wash" or "cook" cash before using it for household purposes, or claim that yams are people, economists must see the response as irrational (it is a metaphor, "noise," or a transaction cost), whereas anthropologists try to understand the context of the statement and illuminate the claim. I overdraw the difference, but economic anthropologists always face a problem: how can we relate diverse forms of economic life to "our" dominant notions of rational choice without disparaging a people's customs and cultural arrangements?

In everyday practices, all of us cross borders, which is a central theme of my book. People erect and then transgress value domains; and in my view, economy consists of disparate value spheres that are juggled and reinvented. To emphasize this theme, I began my book (page 12) with an extended example of the way Panamanian farmers use different measuring rods for their divergent tasks and outcomes. They did not compare them by labor cost or market value or unite them in a meta-scale. I use this notion of value difference within economy throughout the book and offer a model for attending to it. But this model does not cohabit easily with a rational actor analysis, because the rational actor chooses among commensurate items, that is, among things that can be compared along a common measuring rod, whether erected in the actor's mind by a cardinal or ordinal ranking, or presented by a monetary scale. The rational actor in the market has a space in my model, but his domain in which things have been culturally constituted as commensurable varies by economy.

Transgressions by people and the anthropologist make Pålsson Syll uneasy, so he sets up a binary opposition in which he is a scientific realist who seeks deep, true causes, and I am a Kuhnian, relativist, and social constructivist. In his view, I must be a nihilist (but, my heavens, I carry out fieldwork and write). We do have points of agreement, however. Both of us think that standard neoclassical economics is limited in application, that unpredictable innovation creates change and surplus in economies, and that methodological individualism does not provide a unique grounding for elucidating social phenomena. We also agree that anthropology and economics are forms of social science, although we differ about its purposes. Pålsson Syll claims that economists build models after the pattern of the natural sciences. They explain and predict. I doubt that his picture portrays what all economists actually do, because some economists are empiricists and even pragmatists – think of the older institutionalists and Veblen, not to mention contemporary feminist economists. Anthropologists also are divided. Some realists search for "deep structures" (or foundations) in society; the examples range from Lévi-Straussian structuralists, to "componential analysts," to "formalist" economic anthropologists. Others focus on personal narratives and situational analyses. For myself, I am interested in the connection of culture and economy, in local models, and in modes of knowledge. So, I do not agree with his simple opposition or with the unflinching realism that he applies to social action.

Let's summarize and parse Pålsson Syll's realism. First, he believes that society is made up of structures. According to Pålsson Syll, "There exists an independent reality beyond our theories and concepts of it." The task of a social scientist is to unearth this deep structure through the models and ideas he develops. Of course, Pålsson Syll adds, we should never confuse our instruments of knowledge with reality itself, but we can begin to apprehend it through the progressive models we build.

Second, this reality consists of social structures and positions that are "prerequisite" for, as well as "influence" and "dispose," individual practices. Personal actions that follow convention reproduce the structures and positions of society, although actors have a degree of autonomy and freedom from the "limitations" of cultural norms and conventions. Pålsson Syll's epistemology here looks like something a standard neoclassical economist might profess, but there is a difference. Both Pålsson Syll and neoclassical economists presume the existence of invariant units; however, a neoclassical economist usually assumes that the building-block or foundation is the rational actor (as Helgesson observes). Pålsson Syll seems to be an institutionalist who starts with roles and positions, as well as relationships. But even here he does not separate the idea of lasting relationships between people from enduring positions – a distinction that captures the difference between British social anthropology and French structuralism. For example, do we consider the underlying elements of society to be relationships (and relations of relations to follow Lévi-Strauss) or are they discrete positions that become connected in relationships (as the British school used to claim)? Either way, as Pålsson Syll observes, the dichotomy raises the "age-old agent-structure problem." Where is the human agent with desires, intentions, and reflexivity in the midst of this structured social realm? Pålsson Syll does not address this problem that is a consequence of his foundationalism except to say that structure and agent are dialectically related levels of abstraction. Oh, my! Through his sleight of hand we first abstract and reify a difference (agent and structure) only to proclaim it is a dialectical relationship. One reason many anthropologists have abandoned a purely structural approach (in either sense of the term) is because we need to address change, difference, history, and people; and because the binary opposition of structure and agent emerges from our own discourse. In this respect, Pålsson Syll's project is the reverse of anthropology's. He remains solipsistically enclosed in his discourse, whereas exploring other worldviews has been a central interest of many anthropologists. We try to become more reflexive about our own knowledge through knowing unfamiliar forms.

Third, Pålsson Syll's realism has a strong undertow, because he claims that structures have "causal power" and that the task of the social scientist is to find the "generative mechanisms that rule a phenomenon" and explain it. When Pålsson Syll claims that events and structures "act" in society, I do not know if his statement reflects a translation problem or his view. Either way, I do not think that structures act, and I am very dubious about attributing underlying causal power to them, or even talking about causality, which remains a diverse and contested concept. So, our paths diverge.

Fourth, Pålsson Syll urges that when the social scientist provides an explanation of social phenomena (such as a high unemployment rate) he is offering a critique of these conditions, by suggesting how through his explanation they can be avoided. But, and this is the fifth segment of Pålsson Syll's realism, the social scientist must also provide a critique of competing explanations by explaining how they are caused by false beliefs. So, by Pålsson Syll's epistemology we have a potpourri of notions including explanation, truth, and morality (good and bad social conditions), critiques, causes, and dialectics, as well as discrete structures. I do note, again, that Pålsson Syll does not critique his own realist assumptions (his lack of reflexivity), and that if I hold false beliefs, then – by his lights – he should have explained why I hold them. Anyway, I am not certain who is supposed to judge true and false, although Pålsson Syll is clear about the latter: it's a question of realist science.

Pålsson Syll conflates events in the "natural" and "social" worlds and applies a contested model of the natural sciences to social action. In the Enlightenment tradition, he says, social reality is independent of our views, because structures, which are independent of our knowledge and beliefs, govern it. But does a stream of water that runs downhill – to use his example – have intentions and images, learn, converse with others, and reflect and change its purposes?

Let's take this part of his argument in stages by asking first what persuades us that a scientific or realistic explanation of objective reality is true. Pålsson Syll offers three ways to justify an explanation. He believes, first, in common sense: we know an explanation is valid when we are able to say "That's right! That explains it." Here we see the extreme form of Pålsson Syll's solipsism. Perhaps he has in mind mathematical intuition. But given Hume's skepticism and Mill's observation that appeals to self-evidence may serve to legitimate vested interests, Pålsson Syll's grounding for judging true statements should leave us unsatisfied. It provides an even less firm basis in light of anthropology, because a century of anthropological studies suggests that "common sense" and intuition vary by culture, context, and social position (Geertz 1983; Herzfeld 2001). If everything is just commonsensical, then anthropologists should fold their tents because there is nothing to explicate! A realist approach to social life needs a more persuasive foundation than an appeal to common sense. Pålsson Syll also adheres to a "counterfactual causal analysis" of truth when he says that "one has to consider whether the event would have taken place even if the factor did not exist." Unfortunately, he does not discuss how this operation can be put to work in real economies. Should we re-run history in order to omit a single "variable"? Need I add that proving "correspondence" between facts and theories is not without stumbling blocks? Finally, Pålsson Syll says that an explanation is true when it has "practical significance." A true explanation offers good grounding for practices or, to use the appropriate term, it has utility. So, Pålsson Syll ultimately grounds his realism on means-to-ends reasoning or that of the rational actor. But now my head is spinning, because Pålsson Syll seems to reject methodological individualism only to reintroduce the Benthamite model of means-to-ends figuring when justifying his methodological structuralism.

One great Vichean insight was that because we make ourselves we can know or understand ourselves in a way that we can never understand a natural object such as a river. Admittedly, the border is fuzzy, as sociobiologists might claim, but the Vichean perspective leads to a different set of questions. For example, most anthropologists see human action as "meaningful" and one of their tasks as reaching an "understanding" of human action. At one stage in their history, anthropologists focused on the problem of "translation." Can ethnographers translate between cultural categories? Today, many are interested in "interpreting" practices and discourse, as well as identities and subjectivities. Divergent methods are used, and there are intense differences about how to carry out the project, but it is very different from Pålsson Syll's because the anthropological endeavor starts with practices, looks to illuminate a diversity of local situations (including ours), and does not claim that it can predict given the contingency and uncertainty of agentive behavior.

Pålsson Syll is correct that once we adopt this line, hell breaks loose, because the project also implicates us. I mean something more than that we must be aware of and critique our position in the Western world as "colonizers," as power holders, and as inheritors of knowledge and writers. Rather, our knowledge is part of a "long conversation" (Gudeman and Rivera 1990). We critique our knowledge through the knowledge and practices (or models) presented by others and in reverse. As I shall explain, I have tried to carry this critical view to another stage in *The Anthropology of Economy* by using our subordinated knowledge in a self-critique.

Anthropologists also compare and contrast, and in so doing sometimes discover ways that our knowledge – and theirs – may serve to "rationalize" or legitimate what we think and do. Given this complicated situation in which we try to shed solipsism for reflexivity through a long conversation, I do not presume that our concept of the rational actor or an invariant structure explicates all behavior concerning material goods and services: people have divergent, contradictory practices that they contextually deploy. Pålsson Syll does not want to open the door to these real-world models, because they lack the anchor he craves.

Let's take the argument a step further. I think standard neoclassical economics has a monistic way of considering value. Throughout *The Anthropology of Economy* I provide examples of the incommensurate. I presume that my notion of commensuration refers to the economists' idea that a rational actor's preferences are complete, continuous, and transitive, as Helgesson observes. The rational actor can compare all the options (Hausman 1992:15). But anthropological evidence suggests this model is an idealization or abstraction. By asking people to rank outcomes and means, we can force them to commensurate, and then assume they are rational, but people do not always act in this fashion: why else do anthropologists find "spheres of exchange" in which transactions are separated into domains? Why else in our economy do we worry about selling body parts, selling national treasures, or selling our bodies for sex? Why else do we set up household budgets so that we do not conflate educational expenditures with buying champagne?

As an anthropologist, I also observe that a large volume of production, distribution, and consumption of material things and services occurs outside markets, for example through households and states (Bowles and Edwards 1993:99). I term this economic space "community," although different words could be used. One of my purposes in the book was to describe some economic processes that occur in this realm. Pålsson Syll suggests that I "conflate economy, culture, and community" and contain "culture and community within economy." Quite the opposite! I think that economy has several faces – mutuality and asocial trade – that are separate and mixed, and I devote one chapter to showing how objects pass between these spaces, sometimes smoothly, sometimes at moral cost. Both the objects and spaces are transformed in the process, and we invent stories to explain why it can happen. Today, with heightened flows of financial capital, goods, and services crossing national boundaries, and the spread of commensuration, we are witnessing more local (moral and social) reactions, such as the rise of barter clubs, the use of local monies, the emergence of cooperatives, and terrorism. Pålsson Syll suggests I falsely dissolve "the tensions and dialectics that signify these different entities" [community and market, local and global]; to the contrary, I recognize and provide a way of exploring them.

HORNBORG'S WORLD

I must address the epistemology of Hornborg rather differently from that of Pålsson Syll. I disagree with Pålsson Syll, but his critiques of me are consistent with his universalist position. In Hornborg's case, his critiques are inconsistent with his announced view. Hornborg values "relativism" but clings to an essentialist view. His criticisms and occasional misreadings of what I wrote are linked to his contradictory approach.

Hornborg distinguishes between the material and the symbolic, or the substantial and the mental. Each makes up a level that we must not confuse. For example, Hornborg opposes the "abstract" to the concrete as a real division (to the detriment of the former). Equally, Hornborg asks that I distinguish between moral symbols of identity and a people's sources of material maintenance. Similarly, he asks me to separate a people's propensity to adopt irreplaceable reference points in their social lives from their recognition of common resources that also provide aspects of identity. Hornborg even projects this division on the difference between formalist and substantivist economic anthropologists: the former engage in the "politics of abstraction," whereas the latter start with the concrete. Finally, and most importantly, Hornborg can endorse "radical relativism" in the human world, because it is disconnected from the law-governed, material world. I do not know what he means by relativism, but certainly he does not explore how we constitute the world for action and in understandings.

I suggest that Hornborg's binary opposition of the mental and the material is part of a modern discourse by which we separate the rule-governed "natural" world from the social world: sometimes we project our constructs about the material world on the social world (as does Pålsson Syll), sometimes we envision them as distinct domains (as does Hornborg), and sometimes we project our social constructs on the material world (as do the Physiocrats). For example, I do not agree with Hornborg that the second law of thermodynamics is "non-ideological," whatever Hornborg intends by that term. (Is it outside human interests?) The second law is a construction or model that we use for certain purposes. In *Conversa-*

tions in Colombia (1990), my co-author and I suggested that the local (Latin American) people's idea of the "strength" (*la fuerza*) of the earth may have an historical connection to an earlier European folk idea about the strength or force of the land, and that conceivably the latter was adopted in European high discourse where it became "force" and "energy" in physics and "utility" in economics (see Mirowski 1989). Reflecting on this possible series of connections or genealogy helps us to see the resilience of the binary opposition, as well as traveling social constructions, but it does not suggest that the notion of force in thermodynamics provides a master or privileged narrative against which all cultures may be seen as relative.

Hornborg mistakenly invokes the division between formalist and substantivist economic anthropology as an example of the divide between the abstract and the concrete, or between the master narrative and the relative. In contrast to Hornborg, I argue that substantivism can be seen as a master narrative, to use Hornborg's label. Karl Polanyi (1944), who authored the opposition, constantly claimed that land and labor were the fundaments of all economies and societies, although their uses differed through history and across societies. On Polanyi's account, land and labor are functionally related to or embedded in other parts of society, through reciprocity and redistribution. For this reason, Polanyi decried the sale or disembedding of land and labor in the market as if they were commodities: this act transforms and destroys society from within, for society cannot sell itself and survive. In effect, Polanyi argued that disruption of his foundational picture destroys society. Because land and labor provide the invariants on which his economic typology is built, Polanyi used the term substantivism for his economics that starts from real, material things ("facts") as opposed to the abstractions or "logic" of neoclassical economics. Polanyi's divide neatly fits Hornborg's epistemology according to which the material and symbolic are separated. But land and labor are not givens prior to culture; they are constituted in discourse and practice in highly variant ways. Substantivism certainly calls for contextual understanding of economy, but it is not "concrete" except that it rhetorically invokes concepts that some of us think are concrete, such as land and labor.

HELGESSON'S VOICE

In his contribution, Gert Helgesson develops several themes from *The Anthropology of Economy*, and adds his reservations about the "utility" of neoclassical economics. Neoclassical economics, Helgesson protests, lumps together needs, wishes, ideals, and values. It does not consider identity formation and the achievement of well-being, while it reduces trust relationships to expressions of self-interest. Helgesson also worries that the neoclassical approach provides a narrow notion of human freedom. Like Pålsson Syll he asks that I place the concept of the rational actor within a larger view of reason. I shall elaborate on some of the issues that Helgesson raises, including the shifting difference between needs and wants, and the problematic of choice in relation to commitments. Also, I shall offer a few suggestions about "development" and the place of trust in impersonal trade. Overall, my comments circle around the interaction of mutuality and competitive trade that I describe in the book, and looking at the issues raised by Helgesson in this light helps to clarify my later responses to the quibbles of Hornborg and Pålsson Syll.

In high market economies the terms *needs* and *wants* are used synonymously, but in the ethnography from Latin America, a distinction is drawn between them by use of words such as "necessities" versus "desires" or "luxuries." These categories are linked to community and market. Needs are specified in relation to the base, or what a person requires to maintain herself in relation to others, or what is needed to survive in community. They vary by context and time. Some needs are met through personal work, some are fulfilled by communal distributions, and some are satisfied by trade; for example, in *The Anthropology of Economy* I describe how goods from the communal realm may enter the market to return in different form to meet "needs" or maintain the base, although not all market goods are used in this fashion. This concept of needs as socially and culturally determined contradicts the neoclassical assumption that preferences are individually established, which is precisely one of Helgesson's reservations about standard economics.

Wants or desires, in contrast, are more individually determined, or so we believe. Wants may be induced by emulation and social influences, such as advertising, but usually they are not expressed in the language of community: "want not, lack not" is a dictum for self-sufficiency and separation from the realm of trade. But the border between want and need is porous, especially when wants are re-presented or dressed up as needs through advertising. Market actors often draw on images of community to attract buyers, as in the case of beer commercials that display its convivial use. From the perspective of community this inducement to buy a want as if it were a need is a mystification. Similarly, we sometimes justify or tell ourselves a story that a want is really a need. By telling ourselves that we need a Lexus rather than a Honda, we legitimate a large expenditure of cash for transportation. This "need" to tell ourselves a story about a purchase suggests that the image of community has a presence in and provides support for market life, just as markets re-form communities.

I would also distinguish the concept of well-being from the standard of living. If standard of living is focused on goods and services, and can be measured across economies by calculations, such as yearly income or average purchasing power, well-being is a qualitative judgment in relation to a community; it is a local concept about people-in-relationships. I am interested in these distinctions – needs and wants, well-being and standard of living – partly because they relate to divergent views about the purpose of "development" to which I turn at the end of my book.

Does development mean a rising standard of living or enhanced well-being? Of course, indices of living standards may include measures that have to do with well-being, such as infant mortality and life expectancy rates, but improvement in these standards is often attributed to market expansion and economic growth.[3] The meaning of welfare is equally unclear. Does it refer to the availability of schooling, to literacy, to psychological health, or to a combination of factors? More important, who defines local welfare – an international agency, a nation, or a community? Let me sketch an approach to the development issue in terms of market and community, and from a macro- and micro-perspective.

The major global development institutions today are the International Monetary Fund (IMF) and the World Bank (WB). Other groups are certainly involved, such as nongovernmental organizations (NGOs), the World Trade Organization (WTO), and national governments. The IMF and the WB have different agendas and projects with varying influence on local life. Aiming to implement growth through macroeconomic and structural changes, the International Monetary Fund loans money to nations, offers technical assistance, and monitors ("surveys") performance according to financial indices, such as a nation's balance of payment and debt position. Two purposes of the IMF are to promote exchange rate stability and eliminate foreign exchange restrictions that hamper world trade.[4] The IMF operates in the financial sphere of economy, and in a recent critique of its operations, Joseph Stiglitz (2002) observed that it principally represents the

[3] For an interesting discussion of the presumed link between per capita gross domestic product and other dimensions of living, see Easterlin 2000.

[4] This information is drawn from the IMF's articles of agreement, under "Purposes" as stated in Article I. The material can be found on the IMF website (www.imf.org).

interests of finance ministers and international bankers. He argues that the IMF adheres to a strict view of "market fundamentalism" (2002:221), and that its advocacy of "capital account liberalization was *the single most important factor leading to the* [recent Asian financial] *crisis*" (2002:99). In the model I offer in the book, the IMF focuses on the abstracted domain of economy in which money trades for itself at a specified interest rate. Whether this concentration on capital flows leads to greater wellbeing or even rising standards of living is questionable.[5]

The World Bank, in contrast, supports local projects that are supposed to have sustainable economic, social, and environmental benefits.[6] With its mandate, the WB promotes efforts that enhance health, education, the environment, public sector governance, and economic sustainability. In recent years, the World Bank has turned to use of local-level information, to recognizing the desires of local communities, and to designing projects that meet basic needs or alleviate poverty. But when evaluating proposals, the WB specifies that a project must have a quantifiable, overall positive rate of return, which is often justified through the attribution of shadow prices. Like the IMF, it employs the language of the market and rational actor to judge where its financial and technical support will be directed. The World Bank commensurates or re-

[5] For an earlier on-the-ground account of the way the IMF operates, with experts flying in and out of a country and cooking unreliable figures, without any local knowledge, so that a country can receive loans, see Klitgaard 1990.

[6] See www.worldbank.org for information about the WB.

duces to a common standard social benefits. In Helgesson's terms, wishes, desires, ideals, and social relationships are leveled out and assessed against a single measuring rod. This position that everything can be compared using top-down technical devices such as cost benefit ratios, measurement of externalities, and assessment of trade-offs reflects the market desire to find a "bottom line," and it conflicts with the politics and voices of local communities in which diverse, "bottom-up" values are formed, contested, and not necessarily measured against one another. Both the IMF and the WB are "fundamentalist" institutions that do not start from positions of epistemological or economic diversity.

In place of these macro-perspectives, let us consider economies as being diverse with multiple aims. For example, in pursuit of "development," an economy might emphasize increasing productivity, raising financial profits, or improving market efficiency; it could aim for full employment, high educational attainment, or the eradication of poverty. Fostering development also could mean putting in place a transparent system of property rights, loaning money, or supporting individual projects. But these goals are market centered, and development could also mean enhancing well-being and the capacity to innovate or exercise human agency. Some innovations are stimulated by market competition, but they take place in the communal realm as well and are supported by it, for innovations build on a legacy of knowledge and emerge through mutuality. In the book, I demonstrate with examples that innovation is not a function of rational calculation but is fostered through the use of various modes of reason, and by interaction and communication, within and between communities. Today, internet use may increase the emergence of innovations; for example, Castells argues that innovation, which is "the primordial function" of the internet, is becoming the product of this "collective intellect" (2001:100 and 101).[7] I propose that enhancing this capacity for innovating new social relationships, goods, and services be a central focus of development efforts.

Development means helping people to build a base that supports mutuality and survival. I have sometimes harbored the view that Cuba, with its achievements in education, health, and a sense of national identity, has fashioned a shared base through which a defined market arena could be sustained (which would be a reversal of the usual imagined historical trajectory). But base building is slow, and not a "quick fix" process. To foster this side of development we need to do more than invest in human, social, and cultural "capital," not to speak of placing constraints on government deficits, inflation, and exchange rates in return for a loan. Visualizing this form of development will require new forms of "assistance" and criteria, with greater respect for the capacities and capabilities of others. It requires a concept of economy as a combination of mutuality and impersonal trade. For example, consider what happens when a squatter settlement forms in an urban area. The inhabitants often arrive from separate areas and have no affiliations; but soon they may

[7] For both an older and more recent discussion of innovation, see von Hippel (1998) and Christensen (1997).

band together to demand "basic services" such as potable water, proper sewage, and electricity. They are trying to build a base. If they receive some help and start a base, they may seek to establish other improvements through assistance with housing materials, access roads, and public transportation. The list varies, but in such a case a base is being constructed through which further individual and group efforts are enabled: economic enhancement requires that a shared realm be developed through which a market arena can grow. This view of "economic development" runs counter to the "shock therapy" plan in which a once-and-for-all change is envisioned. My general model can be extended to justify effective and appropriate welfare systems in all economies. The model is not predictive, but it is normative, because economy encompasses moral relations as well as impersonal trade, and it legitimates new discussions about economic purposes.

Finally, I turn to trust, which is a mutual relationship. In a market trade, trust may play several roles, such as insuring that information provided between trading partners is reliable, that debts will be paid, or that adjustments can be made in an open-ended exchange. It means putting many calculations about trusted partners into abeyance, which is its "pay-off." A trust relation does lower transaction costs, so it is rational in the market. But as Helgesson observes, a trust relation presupposes shared values, norms, and promise-keeping. Thus, does trust provide a social framework for the exercise of calculative reason, or is trust a calculated bond itself? Can it be derived from self-interest, because if one calculates a commitment it can be continuously recalculated, which undermines the promise? Trust between partners in the market illustrates the mixed, shifting, and dialectical relation of mutuality and impersonal trade.

The Frafra migrants from northeast Ghana who moved to a shantytown in Accra provide an example of trust in the market. Lacking resources, Keith Hart reports (2000), they became traders who engaged in both licit and illicit activities. But the shantytown dwellers faced a problem. With little capital and access to currency, they often relied on loans and the extension of credit among themselves, so default was an ever-present possibility. Because they existed at the margins of state control and enforcement, legal contracts could not be used, while resort to violence or public shaming were not long-term solutions to the enforcement problem. In the rural area, the Frafra traders had belonged to kinship groups; however, their traditional ethic of sharing would not have fit well with self-interested exchange, and in the city most of the ties that connoted identity, sameness, and a collective self had dissolved. Eventually, through trial and error, and at the cost of time and monetary losses, individual trust relationships emerged. Credit was provided only to these persons, while loans were never offered to strangers, with whom transactions were made on the basis of immediate cash payments. Thus, a loosely structured market space that depended on a network of debits and credits emerged through personal bonds, yet these relationships were instigated by the need and desire to have market trade.

The formation of such trust bonds between traders encapsulates economy's seam between mutuality and self-interest. But this contradictory bond is papered over by economistic analyses in which trust becomes an instrument or tool of rational choice. For example, in a study that draws on the new institutional economics, Landa analyzes ethnic trading networks and gift exchange. She argues that traders, who are profit-maximizers, create institutions to reduce their costs of exchange ("The role of institutions is to economize on transaction costs" [Landa 1994:23]). In place of formal law, traders' institutions, such as ethnic bonds and gift exchange, constrain breaches of contract. One of Landa's main illustrations is the Kula exchange as described by Malinowski (1961 [1922]). The Kula, briefly, consists of two opposite circuits of exchange: armshells are passed in one direction against a flow of necklaces from the other. These open-ended gift exchanges, which involve chains of debts and credits, are connected to local ceremonies, gender relations, productive activities, canoe building, kinship obligations, as well as the achievement of rank and prestige.[8] Since Malinowski, the Kula has been extensively discussed in the anthropological literature, and it was used by Mauss (1990 [1950]) to exemplify the social role of the gift or reciprocity, which he sharply distinguished from market trade. But for Landa, to summarize a long ahistorical argument, "[T]he Kula Ring is an institutional arrangement that emerged primarily in order to economize on transaction costs of intertribal commercial exchange in stateless societies" (Landa 1994:143). In other words, the entire Kula ring or network was a calculated choice of self-interested actors, even

---

[8] See Weiner (1976) for a revision of Malinowski's ethnography and interpretation.

though it is built on reciprocity. I cite Landa not to enter into a discussion of alternative ways of interpreting the Kula but to suggest how through a rational choice analysis, which "explains" the emergence and "function" of institutions, the communal or mutual realm of economy is visualized as derived from the same means-to-ends calculation that fuels market trade. By reducing mutual ties to a rational calculation, communal relationships become instruments for trade and expressions of its innermost dynamic. According to Landa's analysis, calculative reason explains both market trade and the communal institutions that surround it. But if so, we may ask, what explains institutional and cultural differences across societies except history or "path dependence" on which instrumental reason operates? And what determines this earlier historical trajectory except previous rational calculations? When all choices are brought to a common measuring rod and evaluated by the standard of efficiency, we cannot understand social and cultural difference. The general argument, of which there are many varieties, is foundationalist, filled with levels, and comforting to those caught within that solipsistic epistemology.

In contrast to Landa and other new institutionalists, I argue that market trust and other transaction commitments – whether enshrined in laws or expressed by networks of producers, merchants, and buyers – are not fully explicable by or reducible to a rational choice foundation. Trust concerns expectations about the reliability of another's words and intentions, and confidence in the dependability of one's own. Trust, built through persuasion, is a commitment that has a fragile if not contradictory relation to the self-interested acts that it ensures.

HORNBORG SPEAKS

Hornborg reserves some of his acerbic words for my use of the term community, for speaking about imagined solidarities, for my purported abandoning of the anthropological project of "de-familiarization," and for my lack of attention to environmental issues. I disagree. To begin, I used the word community for people who share common interests and mutuality. I cannot imagine community as anything other than "imagined," even when it is "up-close"! Thus, I purposely extended the word to cover "broad" and "thin" associations, such as an alumni group, as well as face-to-face situations. Siblings share something, as do members of environmental groups; but siblings also may live halfway across the world. We have many communities and identities through them. In community, what people share is their base that partly makes up their identity; it can be "material" or not. Sometimes the base is epitomized as an object or utterance, which I term its sacra. Alienating the base (by turning it to private property) or obliterating the sacra destroys community, because relationships are mediated through them. The community is debased. Hornborg huffs that "anything ... can serve as a common reference point for some kind of social category in some kind of context." Why not, and what has happened to his relativism?

In contrast to what Hornborg claims, I address social or communal identities that are purchased in the market. When we buy and wear a hat that displays a sports star, team logo, or trademark, are we asserting a real or reified affiliation? Either way, through the purchase and use we transform capital, private property, or a commodity to base that asserts mutuality with others. In the market situation, images and metaphors of community seem to provide especially persuasive forms of consumer advertising; the figures of one are reified in the other ("homegrown" orange juice is pervasive in supermarkets). I also discuss how this process occurs in ethnographic contexts when people trade for their sacra and then use it to make relationships. In these and other ways the values of mutuality and asocial trade are separate but intertwined. Non mutual practices and sociality are constitutive of each other. Market and community are not different territories to be exclusively described by a bounded discourse, such as standard economics, but by a broader lexicon.

Hornborg thus fails to see that I have hardly left aside the project of critique and de-familiarization (otherwise why is Pålsson Syll so cross?). I turned the project inward. I do not visualize economic anthropology in terms of a divide between "us" and the "other," or between modern and postmodern situations. I am criticizing asocial exchange through our own practices, or the mutuality that we continuously try to establish in relation to trade. We "relativize" ourselves because we have a divided life with which we continuously struggle. Instead of projecting this division on the world, to separate our modern selves from ethnographic societies by labeling them "exotic" and "pre-modern," I see us as harboring a tension in economy about which the politics of the book spins its web.

Hornborg also inverts my arguments about the distribution of profit. I use the word innovation in relation to profit because it asserts that value is made or constructed through human agency; the assertion may be banal for anthropologists, but it turns economics away from mechanistic and essentialist assumptions about the source of profit in which Hornborg conspires by asserting that energy and raw materials also have the capacity to generate profits (his footnote 7). Innovations provide new models, and because they are nourished in the context of social relationships, I suggest that we should rethink how profits are distributed in the context of community. I further offer that today the innovation capacity seems to be highly protected or kept in industrial centers, unlike farming out production lines and service centers to low-labor-cost areas. I have proposed that development has to do with building this human creative capacity everywhere; but Hornborg reverses my statements by saying I advocate keeping profits in industrial areas. To the contrary, I advocate distributing the capacity to innovate, with all this implies about enhancing education, social supports, and the opportunity to draw on capital resources; and I advocate distributing profits outside the boundaries set by private property because profits are also due to community. More broadly still, I support building local models.

Finally, the concept of the locally specified base, which mixes the material and the mental, is directly applicable to environmental issues. If instead of bounded, private property we think in terms of what we share (such as the ozone layer, the oceans, air, streams, and forests), of the way these commonalities make communities in which we live, and of the identities we fashion in relation to them, then environmental issues become part of the political economy I envision. But Hornborg wants us to attend to these problems through the idea of "natural capital," so accepting and endorsing the standard discourse that he wants me to oppose.

PÅLSSON SYLL'S LAST WORDS OR THE VALUE OF LISTENING TO OTHERS

With this background, we can turn to Pålsson Syll's semantic quibbles. He does not connect his epistemological worries about my anthropology to his criticism of my interpretations of the Physiocrats, Marx, and Schumpeter. But the two parts of his essay are linked, which is why he fails to understand what I said about surplus. Pålsson Syll thinks his realism provides privileged access to older texts so he can refashion them in light of his modern notions. My project is different. I addressed the Physiocratic and Marxist local models as forms of persuasion that contain their own legitimation. I did not explore the contexts of production or acceptance of these texts but rather the cultural narratives or stories the authors adduced to justify their models. Incidentally, to make this story more complex, Marx offered his analysis of Physiocracy. He (1963 [1905–10]) saw Physiocracy as a mystification because it traced the generation of surplus value not to labor but to the earth (1963 [1905–10:52]), which justified the landowner's unearned return. In Marx's view, Physiocracy was a class-based theory; for Pålsson Syll it was an early scientific achievement.

I focused briefly on the Physiocratic model to try to

show how it made sense as an explanatory and normative project. The model was influential in France roughly during the twenty years preceding the French Revolution. Physiocracy means "rule of nature," and in many respects the Physiocrats were influenced by natural law theory and Locke's empiricism, which helps us to understand their endeavor. Quesnay, who was doctor to the King, was the central figure, although Turgot's *Reflections on the Formation and the Distribution of Riches* (1898 [1770]) is a fascinating but mixed document.

The Physiocratic model depicts a three-class society consisting of cultivators (or husbandmen), landowners, and artisans. At the beginning of the agricultural year, the cultivators have sufficient resources to plant. At the end of this cycle they harvest enough to reproduce their labors and costs, and to yield a surplus that was termed the *produit net*. This latter sum flows to the landowners. The cultivators and the landowners use their returns to reproduce their lives and to trade with the artisans who refashion and also consume the raw materials they receive. The only "extra" coming into this circulatory flow emanates from the land (more broadly, nature).

On my interpretation, the Physiocratic model – especially the specification of the *produit net* – was constructed by applying and overlapping three metaphors, all drawn from the human body. First, there was the idea of circulation through the social body, which was probably influenced by the image of the flow of blood in the human body that had been discovered by Harvey. Second, there was the image of reproduction as in the birth process: the cultivator was termed a "husbandman" and not farmer or peasant as Pålsson Syll describes. Third, drawing on the Physiocratic acceptance of natural law theory and empiricism, I suggest that Locke's concept of mind by which external sensation is separate from and prior to internal operations was projected on the relation between nature and society. The three metaphors overlapped in agriculture, which was part of the circulatory system, the location for reproduction of foods, and external to human manipulation. (The artisans were not considered to be productive in the Physiocratic sense. They operated on given materials by combining, joining, and separating them, whereas the husbandmen helped bring them into society.) As Pålsson Syll does observe, in Physiocracy wealth has both a material and value dimension, although he admits that in the *Tableau Économique* Quesnay offered a more material notion (Turgot's essay seems to slide from one to the other halfway through). Schumpeter also observed about Quesnay "[h]e took it for granted that the fact of physical productivity implied value productivity, and he shifted in midstream from one to the other" (1954:238). But Pålsson Syll erases this mixing of "nature" and "value" to reframe Physiocracy as a modern or early modern model.

Pålsson Syll and I differ about the Physiocratic concept of "surplus" or the *produit net*. He projects on their idea our notion of profit and claims that the cultivator, after paying taxes and rents, sells his products at market price and "keeps his profit." Profit, he concludes, "accrues only to the agricultural farmer." Pålsson Syll does not provide a Physiocratic term for profit, nor did he notice that I did not use the word with reference to the Physiocrats.

I wrote "surplus" for *produit net*. This surplus from agriculture covered rent, as well as taxes and other expenditures: it is different from market profit. I was interested in how the Physiocrats explained this extra that provided for accumulation or consumption by the landowners. What was its source, how was it generated?[9] Shall we listen to them?

Mirabeau said "The land is the mother of all goods" and added that wealth comes only from the land (cited in Meek 1963:120–121).

Quesnay and Mirabeau referred to "the spontaneous gifts of nature" (cited in Meek 1963:60).

Quesnay also argued that "[t]he origin, the principle, of all expenditure and all wealth is the fertility of the land, whose products can be increased only through these products themselves"; and he said that agricultural goods are a "true generation or creation of wealth" (1963 [1766]:209, 223).

Turgot said much the same when he claimed that nature provides a "superfluidity" to humans as a "pure gift" (Turgot 1898 [1770]:9, 12, 13, 14, 51).

Actually, Quesnay did not view agriculture as the only productive sphere, for he also said that productive expenditure "could be employed in agriculture, grasslands, pasture, forests, mines, fishing, etc., in order to perpetuate wealth in the form of corn, drink, wood, livestock,

[9] "They had seen the crucial point of framing the question as to the source and explanation of a produit net or surplus … . [A] whole class of landowners in fact lived upon this form of rent of land" (Dobb 1973:40).

raw materials for manufactured goods, etc." (1972 [1758-9]:i).

I observe that Quesnay is addressing productive expenditure in the Physiocratic sense, whereas Pålsson Syll seems to include all expenditures in his analysis of "profit." Note again that for the Physiocrats artisans were not productive, because their activities were "barren" or "sterile" – to use the Physiocratic terms. I remark as well on the wide application of the "reproductive" metaphor through use of expressions such as barren, sterile, fertility, land as mother, and cultivator as husbandman. We should also observe a contradiction in Quesnay's statement about productive expenditure: how could mining be productive in the Physiocratic sense, while livestock were not? Quesnay actually was inconsistent about mining and other Physiocrats disagreed with him, whereas livestock were probably seen as a form of traction (Weulersse 1931:277–280). Such "cultural" queries help reveal the limits of the model.

But now we come to the center point of my difference with Pålsson Syll. I take seriously Turgot's statements that agricultural returns are a "gift of nature" and that the land provides a "pure gift to him who cultivates it" (1898 [1770]:14, 89). Whereas I suggest how this notion fits with other Physiocratic expressions, Pålsson Syll dismisses the statements as "metaphorical"! Well, he's right. But models often elaborate an initial metaphor, and what's wrong with using a metaphor – or a model? They can be persuasive.

The reader will also see that Pålsson Syll and I use the word *surplus* differently. I employ it in a more Marxist sense to refer to the generation of an "extra" that may be divided into rents, profits, taxes, tithes, interest, and other deductions, and I am interested in how it is generated – or, rather, how people explain and legitimate its generation. Pålsson Syll equates surplus with money profit. I wish the economist had noted the local or people's uses.

With respect to Marx, Pålsson Syll again misconstrues my cultural project as well as what Marx stated. Clearly, as Pålsson Syll says, in capitalism the size of profit that the capitalist secures varies with the class struggle. When the wage or exchange-value of labor is depressed, profits rise; and when the exchange-value of labor rises, profits fall. Similarly, when the working day is lengthened, profit rises, just as it falls when the working day is shortened – all assuming no change in productivity. This inverse relationship is expressed by the rate of exploitation (which is profits [or surplus] divided by wages [or the exchange-value of labor]). But what is new in this formulation? Ricardo had presaged this construction of the class struggle. We can also, as both Pålsson Syll and Hornborg assert, see the capitalist as gathering a profit by paying the laborer less value than what he creates. Their formulation, however, does not attend to Marx's new distinction between the exchange-value or potential of labor in repose and its use-value or activity. I was addressing this cultural narrative that Marx provides about the source of surplus or of value. For instance, in *Wage-Labour and Capital*, Marx says:

> The labourer receives means of subsistence [i.e., a wage] in exchange for his labour-power; but the cap-

italist receives, in exchange for his means of subsistence, labour, the productive activity of the labourer, the creative force by which the worker not only replaces what he consumes, but also *gives to the accumulated labour a greater value than it previously possessed.* (1976 [1847]:31)

Likewise, in *Capital*, Marx writes that labour-power (or labor in action) is "*a source not only of value, but of more value than it has itself*" (1967 [1867]:193).

In his masterful study, Kolakowski also explains that a capitalist can make money because

[t]here exists on the market a particular commodity [i.e. labour-power] whose use-value [i.e., labour or labour in action] is a *source* of value, and which creates exchange-value [as embodied in a commodity] as its use-value [living labour] is realized, i.e. in the process of consumption. (1978:278; italics added)

Dobb, whom Pålsson Syll also cites, explains the generation of surplus in a similar way:

The "nourishing matter" needed to replace the energy used-up in work was the material input into human labour; and the possibility and dimensions of surplus-value depended upon the value of the former being less than the value "created" as output by the labour it sustained. (1973:150–151)

Finally, in *Capital* Marx states:

The property therefore which labour-power in action, living labour, possesses of preserving value, at the same time that it adds it, is a gift of Nature which costs the

labourer nothing but which is very advantageous to
the capitalist inasmuch as it preserves the existing value
of his capital ... . [T]he capitalist is too much absorbed
in money-grubbing to take notice of this gratuitous
gift of labour. (1967 [1867]:206–207)

When I wrote that Marx sought a foundation for profit
outside the market system, I was referring to this human
ability to produce more value than it needs to survive – a
capacity that is also exercised in ancient, slave, feudal,
and communist modes of production. If humans did not
have this capacity, there would be no accumulation. Even
Pålsson Syll admits to this capacity when he says that
"[v]alue is created in the process of labor, where the value-creating potential of labor power is realized." I do not
know exactly what Marx meant when he described this
capacity as a natural gift, but I should think he was referring to a species capacity. I find it interesting that in *Theories of Surplus Value* (1963:51, see also 49, 52, 55, 57),
Marx criticized Physiocracy in which surplus-value "appears therefore as a *gift of nature*" (referring, of course, to
the land rather than labor). Did he appropriate and transform their language? I do not denigrate Marx's formulation when I say it is a cultural narrative. It has been persuasive, although one might argue that it is a foundationalist story as well as a positioned view – that of the laborer on the factory line.

I doubt it is worthwhile to quibble with Pålsson Syll
over my use of words with respect to the Schumpeterian
notion of innovation and profits, but briefly, I understand
normal profit as the return to the entrepreneur (who is a
composite in today's economy). Super-normal profit re-

fers to profit that would not result in conditions of perfect competition: the excess appears because barriers to entry are erected so that short-run equilibrium is not reached. I discuss other forms of profit as extensions of this model under the general label arbitrage.

Pålsson Syll and I agree about the importance of innovation. My theme was twofold: innovation is not a product of calculative reason or means-to-ends figuring, and in this sense falls outside the realm of pure market trade; it also involves reason nourished in and through social relations and a heritage, or in community. Pålsson Syll agrees, and even suggests that I offer an improvement on Schumpeter's economistic approach. Pålsson Syll also suggests that I omit the element of serendipity when considering the innovation process, and I agree that this aspect of innovation should have been more strongly underlined, although in my example of the Guatemalan potter that he admires, I show how serendipity affects her products (Gudeman 2001:111–112). I agree with both Pålsson Syll and Helgesson that we need a more fine-tuned account of reason, which should be part of economics. For example, humans employ dialectical and deductive reason as well as reflexive reason. We draw on figurative reason, using both metaphor and synecdoche to formulate practices. Trial-and-error pragmatic action might be counted as a combination of reasoned processes if not a mode of reason itself. And the ability to disconnect and join, to fragment and combine, is a form of human rationality, as Locke (1975 [1690]) and Diderot (1751), among others, observed; this analytical, critical, and combinatorial faculty, which supports innovation, builds connections between means and ends. All these reasoning processes are nurtured and honed through social relationships or community. As part of this larger view of reason, the calculative form, enshrined in the solitary rational actor, takes its place but is not the only form of reason used in economy.

In this short essay, I have been suggesting how mutuality expressed through shared and contested values, cultural stories, as well as local resistance to and acceptance of pure trade is part of economy: household economies, cooperatives, savings associations, and many other mutual associations have economic tasks, but they are not reducible to a universal model based on calculative reason. Economy is not a singular bounded space but locally intertwines sociality and impersonal exchanges whose combination can energize innovations. The outcome is uncertain and unpredictable. But we seem to have discursively separated this interweaving into the sterile opposition of markets and capitalism versus socialism and communism – each of which becomes a hermetic or solipsistic model. I argue for giving up the search for essentials and foundations that characterize one series of models, and for opening a long conversation or creative dialogue among the many that we find. This approach is not radical relativism but a positive program that leads to comparison, critique, reflexivity, and enhanced human communication in the search for freedom. If Pålsson Syll wishes to conclude that by offering an argument about economic behavior as local, I have fallen "into the postmodern abyss of relativism," I can only ask: who says I must accept his epistemology and rhetoric? What makes it the finality?

Pålsson Syll's "realism," one might observe, becomes his cover story or hegemonic move to validate re-reading earlier thinkers and contemporary ethnography in light of his "modern" theories. But is it not "just" a cultural narrative? After all, we do create cultural stories to "explain" ourselves to ourselves, to explain others to ourselves, and to legitimate our actions and writing.

REFERENCES

Becker, Gary S. 1981. *A Treatise on the Family*. Cambridge: Harvard University Press.

Bowles, Samuel, and Richard Edwards. 1993. *Understanding Capitalism*, 2nd ed. New York: HarperCollins.

Castells, Manuel. 2001. *The Internet Galaxy*. Oxford: Oxford University Press.

Christensen, Clayton M. 1997. *The Innovator's Dilemma: When New Technologies Cause Great Firms to Fail*. Boston: Harvard Business School Press.

Diderot, Denis. 1751. "Art," *Encyclopédie, ou Dictionnaire Raisonné des Sciences, des Artes et des Métiers*, eds. Denis Diderot and Jean le Rond d'Alembert, vol. I, pp. 713–717. Paris: Briasson, David, Le Breton, Durand.

Dobb, Maurice. 1973. *Theories of Value and Distribution since Adam Smith*. Cambridge: Cambridge University Press.

Easterlin, Richard A. 2000. "The Worldwide Standard of Living since 1800," *Journal of Economic Perspectives*, vol. 14, no. 1, pp. 7–26.

Geertz, Clifford. 1983. *Local Knowledge*. New York: Basic Books.

Gudeman, Stephen. 1986. *Economics as Culture*. London: Routledge.

Gudeman, Stephen, and Mischa Penn, 1982. "Models, Meanings and Reflexivity," *Semantic Anthropology*, ed. David Parkin, pp. 89–106. London: Academic Press.

Gudeman, Stephen, and Alberto Rivera. 1990. *Conversations in Colombia*. Cambridge: Cambridge University Press.

Hart, Keith. 2000. "Kinship, Contract, and Trust: The Economic Organization of Migrants in an African City Slum," *Trust: Making and Breaking Cooperative Relations*, ed. Diego Gambetta, electronic edition, Department of Sociology, University of Oxford, chapter 6, pp. 176–193, http://www.sociology.ox.ac.uk/papers/hart176-193.pdf.

Hausman, Daniel M. 1992. *The Inexact and Separate Science of Economics*. Cambridge: Cambridge University Press.

Herzfeld, Michael. 2001. *Anthropology: Theoretical Practice in Culture and Society*. Malden: Blackwell Publishers.

Klitgaard, Robert. 1990. *Tropical Gangsters*. New York: Basic Books.

Kolakowski, Leszek. 1978. *Main Currents of Marxism*, vol. 1. Oxford: Oxford University Press.

Landa, Janet Tai. 1994. *Trust, Ethnicity, and Identity*. Ann Arbor: University of Michigan Press.

Locke, John. 1975 [1690]. *An Essay Concerning Human Understanding*, ed. Peter H. Nidditch. Oxford: Clarendon Press.

Malinowski, Bronislaw. 1961 [1922]. *Argonauts of the Western Pacific*. New York: Dutton.

Marx, Karl. 1967 [1867]. *Capital* (vol. 1). New York: International Publishers.

—. 1963 [1905-10]. *Theories of Surplus-Value*, Part I. Moscow: Progress Publishers.

—. 1976 [1847]. *Wage-Labour and Capital*. New York: International Publishers.

Mauss, Marcel. 1990 [1950]. *The Gift*. London: Routledge.

Meek, Ronald L. 1963. *The Economics of Physiocracy: Essays and Translations*. Cambridge, Mass.: Harvard University Press.

Mirowski, Philip. 1989. *More Heat than Light*. Cambridge: Cambridge University Press.

Polanyi, Karl. 1944. *The Great Transformation*. Boston: Beacon Press.

—. 1968. *Primitive, Archaic and Modern Economies*, ed. George Dalton. Garden City: Anchor Books.

Quesnay, Francois. 1972. [1758-9]. *Tableau Économique*, trans. and ed. Marguerite Kucynski and Ronald L. Meek. London: Macmillan.

Ruttan, Vernon W. 2003. *Social Science Knowledge and Economic Development*. Ann Arbor: University of Michigan Press.

Schumpeter, Joseph A. 1954. *History of Economic Analysis*. New York: Oxford University Press.

Stiglitz, Joseph E. 2002. *Globalization and Its Discontents*. New York: W.W. Norton & Co.

Turgot, Anne Robert Jacques, Baron de l'Aulne. 1898 [1770]. *Reflections on the Formation and the Distribution of Riches*. New York: Macmillan & Co.

Hippel, Eric von. 1998. *The Sources of Innovation*. New York: Oxford University Press.

Weiner, Annette B. 1976. *Women of Value, Men of Renown*. Austin: University of Texas Press.

Weulersse, Georges. 1931. *Les Physiocrates*. Paris: G. Doin.

CONTRIBUTORS

STEPHEN GUDEMAN, professor of anthropology at the University of Minnesota, has carried out fieldwork in Panama, Colombia, and Guatemala and has made short field studies elsewhere. His interests range from religion, beliefs, and the social realm to material life. For a number of years he has been developing a cultural approach to economy that is comparative and cross-disciplinary; it applies to ethnographic contexts as well as formal theory. The author of five books and numerous articles on these and related subjects, Gudeman has been a press and journal editor and has held various offices in organizations in his discipline. He has taught at a number of universities in the U.S. and abroad, has lectured extensively, and has been a member of several institutes for advanced study. In 2002–2003, he was a fellow at the Swedish Collegium for Advanced Study in the Social Sciences, in Uppsala.

GERT HELGESSON is a researcher at the Centre for Bioethics at Karolinska Institutet and Uppsala University, his main focus at present being research ethics, particularly issues concerning informed consent. As a doctoral student at the Department of Philosophy, Uppsala University, Helgesson participated in the interdisciplinary research project "Ethical Reflection in Economic Theory and Practice," which included economists, philosophers, and theological ethicists. During that time he edited the book series *Studies in Ethics and Economics*, which covered a lively debate between economists and philosophers. Helgesson's dissertation, *Values, Norms and Ideology in Mainstream Economics* (2002), addresses the question of whether neoclassical microeconomics is a value-free science. He has also written on ethical aspects of economic theory in "Economics and ethics," published in Øygarden (ed.), *Economism in Our Time* (in Swedish, 2001).

ALF HORNBORG received his PhD in cultural anthropology from Uppsala University in 1986 and became associate professor of anthropology in 1989. Since 1993 he has been professor and chair of the Human Ecology Division at Lund University. He has conducted fieldwork in Peru, Canada, and Tonga. His primary regional interest is in the indigenous and Pre-Columbian cultures of South America. Theoretically and thematically, his research interests have included comparative studies of kinship, spatial symbolism, personhood, human-environmental relations, economic systems, unequal exchange, and processes of capital accumulation in world systems. He is the author of *Dualism and Hierarchy in Lowland South America* (1988 [1986]) and *The Power of the Machine: Global Inequalities of Economy, Technology, and Environment* (2001), as well as numerous articles in scientific journals, the most recent of which is "Ethnogenesis, Regional Integration, and Ecology in Prehistoric Amazonia: Toward a System Perspective" (*Current Anthropology*, August 2005).

STAFFAN LÖFVING is assistant professor at the Institute of Latin American Studies, Stockholm University. His ongoing research deals with paramilitarism and the changing face of state power and civil violence in Latin America (see, e.g., "Paramilitaries of the Empire: Guatemala, Colombia and Israel," *Social Analysis*, Spring 2004). His doctoral research explored the perspectives of revolutionary Maya peasants and post-war discourses on ideology and culture in Guatemala and within anthropology. The dissertation, *An Unpredictable Past: Guerrillas, Mayas, and the Location of Oblivion in Post-war Guatemala*, was defended in 2002 at the Department of Cultural Anthropology and Ethnology, Uppsala University. He is the co-author (with Charlotta Widmark) of *Banners of Belonging: The Politics of Indigenous Identity in Bolivia and Guatemala* (2002).

LARS PÅLSSON SYLL received a PhD in economic history in 1991 and a PhD in economics in 1997, both from Lund University. He became associate professor in economic history in 1995. Since 2004 he has been professor of civics at Malmö University. His primary research areas have been in the philosophy and methodology of economics, theories of distributive justice, and critical realist social science. He is the author of *Utility Theory and Structural Analysis* (1997), *Economic Theory and Method: A Critical Realist Perspective* (in Swedish, 2001), *The History of Economic Theories* (in Swedish, third ed.

2002), as well as numerous articles in scientific journals. At present his research focuses on multiculturalism and globalization.